Table of content

E Collar Training

Everything You Need to Know to Effectively Train Your Dog with an E Collar

PUPPY TRAINING

A Step By Step Guide to Positive Puppy Training That Leads to Raising the Perfect, Happy Dog, Without Any of the Harmful Training Methods!

E Collar Training

Everything You Need to Know to Effectively Train Your Dog with an E Collar

Introduction

Congratulations on purchasing *E Collar Training,* and thank you for doing so.

The following chapters will discuss all of the things that you need to know when it comes to e collar training. There is a lot of controversy out there when it comes to this kind of training. Some dog owners are big proponents of this training method, saying it was the most effective and fast method for them to train their dog to behave, even when they are not there. And on the other side of things, plenty of dog owners feel that this training method falls flat and that it is not the best for any dog owner to work with.

While it is true that the e collar should not be the only training method that you use with your dog, and in fact, it should be used in conjunction with some other training methods as well, there is no denying the progress that can come when you want to fight off some disruptive behaviors with your dog quickly. This guidebook is going to go over the basics of e collar training, how to pick out a good collar, how to be safe with this collar, and even some of the steps that you can use to teach your dog how to behave with this collar.

The first part of this guidebook is going to explore all of the things that you need to know when it comes to the e collar. We will look at some of the basics of the e collar and how to use it safely, some of the benefits and potential drawbacks that come with this kind of collar, and even the accessories that are needed to make sure that it works right. We will also explore a bit about how to properly fit the collar on the dog, and how to make sure you get the right stimulation for your dog to ensure they feel and respond to it, without causing the dog any harm or pain along the way.

Next, we will take a look at some of the different training techniques that you are able to use with this collar. We will explore the steps that you need to use when it comes to off-leash training and perimeter training, and even some of the basics about using commands with the training, or when you should just rely on the collar for the best results.

The end of this guidebook will help us to learn a bit more about the basics of e collar training. We will talk about some of the forms of correction that you can use with this collar, how to handle some of the different distractions that your dog may face, and then answer some of the most common questions that dog owners have when it comes to using and seeing results with this kind of collar on their dog.

Training your dog is a process that takes some time and some patience along the way. Whether you are just trying to get a good head start with your training or you have a bad behavior that has appeared in your dog, and you want to get it taken care of sooner rather than later, the e collar may be the right choice to add into your training methods. When you are ready to learn a bit more about e collar training and some of the benefits, as well as the steps that you need to know to get started, make sure to check out this guidebook today!

There are plenty of books on this subject on the market, thanks again for choosing this one! Every effort was made to ensure it is full of as much useful information as possible. Please enjoy!

Chapter 1: The Tools That You Need for E Collar Training

When it comes to training your puppy, there are a lot of different options that you can choose from. Often working with treats and praise, and other rewards will be the trick that your puppy needs to learn. Others want to find methods that are a bit faster because they are short on time or won't be able to stay home and deal with properly training their puppy. And others may need to deal with some problem areas with their dog, and they need to find something new that will help them out.

There are a ton of tools that you can use, and you can consider which method is going to work the best for you. But here, we are going to explore the idea of the e collar and why it may be the choice that you need to help with training your puppy and getting them to behave in the manner that you would like.

What is the E Collar?

Before we start to look at some of the particulars that come with the e collar, we first need to explore what this device really is. An e collar is going to be an electronic collar or a shock collar, that can help you to properly train your puppy to act in the manner that you would like. There are some pet owners who are not fond of these because they feel that it is not effective, that they are providing a shortcut that doesn't help with the bond between a dog and their owner, and they worry that these collars are going to be painful for the puppy.

Despite some of these claims, you will find that the e collar is not going to be painful, and it can be a really good method of raining your puppy to act in the manner that you want. There are actually a lot of benefits and arguments that go for the use of the e collar, and maybe some of them are the reason why you decided to work with the e collar in the first place. Some of the arguments for using these e collars with training your puppy will include:

1. They are not going to be any different than other forms of training. There are some dog trainers who will use the e collar and who claim that when used properly, the stimulus from the collar is going to be no different than a little tug on the leash or something similar that you may use with your puppy.

2. The technology that goes with these e collars has improved over the years. When these were first invented, it was impossible to adjust the shock level. The ones that are made today can be adjusted based on the type of dog you have and how much you want to use it. The lowest level of these is so low that even a small dog won't be able to fit it. You can adjust the level so that it annoys your dog, but it won't cause harm.

3. For some types of dogs, these collars are going to be the most effective way to train them. Trainers who decide to use these collars are going to claim that certain types of dogs are going to respond better to a stimulus from the collar than from other types of reinforcement.

Before you jump on board and decide to use the e collar for your needs, there are a few things that you should consider. Always remember that while this can be a good training tool in some cases, you have to use it responsibly, and you have to remember that it is not going to work for all dogs. Taking care to determine if it is working for your dog and if it is the right option for you is going to make a bit difference.

The first thing to consider when you want to work with this kind of collar is to remember it should not be the only training tool that you use. There is a ton of evidence out there that points to how positive stimuli for your dog is going to be more effective when you are trying to train them. Rewarding your dog with some treats or another reward when they perform the right behavior, teaching them what the word no means, and using verbal commands work well for most dogs.

If you are using these options in the proper manner, you will probably find that the use of the e collar can be limited for just a few behaviors that the dog does, and you can't seem to break. For example, if you have trouble with them barking all of the time, or they have some leash aggression, you can use the collar to help out with those problems. But for other types of commands and other parts of your training, consider taking the collar off and using other methods.

Another thing to watch out for is whether you have a dog that is aggressive or not. If you find that your dog is more on the aggressive side, the collar is not going to be the best. If you start to train without the collar, and you find that during those sessions, the dog becomes more aggressive when you scold them, then they are not going to respond the best to the shock, no matter how low the level is. aggressive dogs are not going to do well with this kind of collar, and you will need to pick another training method.

Once you have determined that the shock collar is going to be the best option for you, check out a few options, and determine which collar is going to be the best for your needs. There are three different types of these e collars that you are able to choose from including obedience collars, bark collars, and containment systems. Each of these is going to be a bit different, so you will need to choose the one that will work the best for your training needs.

First, let's take a look at the containment system and the barking collars. These are going to provide the stimulus automatically to the dog when they do whatever behavior they are not supposed to do. Obedience collars are a bit different in that they have a remote so that the trainer is able to be in control over the stimulus and can decide when to use it and when not to.

Your goal with using this kind of collar is going to be to find a comfortable shock setting that works the best for your dog. The key here is to find the level of stimulus that is going to be high enough that it gets your dog to pay attention to it, but still low enough that it won't end up causing the dog any pain. A good indicator of this is going to be when you press the button for the collar, you should see the dog perk up their ears and turn their head like they are saying "What was that?"

If you are using the collar and they yelp or put their tail between their legs, this is a sign that the shock is too strong for the dog. A good way to make sure that you can get the right stimulus level of your dog is to pick out one collar that is going to have a high number of stimulation levels so that you can choose the best level that will be effective without hurting the dog. You can also choose to hold the collar to your hand to test the different levels of vibration to see what is best for them.

You can also pick out a collar that is going to beep. Most of the e collars that you are able to pick out will also have the option of delivering a beep along with the shock. If the dog starts to associate the beef with that negative stimulus, you may find that the beeping will be enough to control the behavior you want without even needing to use a shock. You will need to use the shock to start with, but over time, you can switch over to just using the beeps instead.

As you are using the collar with the remote, try to hide the remote as much as possible. If your dog starts to see the remote and they associate it with the shock, they are going to start having a fear of the remote control, and in some cases, they are going to be more aggressive to it. They will associate the remote as the bad thing, rather than seeing that their negative behavior is the reason they are getting that stimulus.

As with any kind of training method that you try to use with your dog, you need to be the responsible one. If you use this electronic training, the most important thing to remember is to use the collar in a responsible manner. Watch the training videos that come with the particular collar that you decide to work with so that you are sure that you are really using it in the proper manner.

The goal of the e collar is to teach the dog how you would like them to behave. You want to give them a little bit of shock that is annoying but not one that is going to harm them. You want it to be a way to get them to pay attention and start changing up the behaviors that they use, but not something that they use all of the time. In fact, it may be something that you only use outside, for example, to make sure the puppy listens to you or doesn't bark to other people and animals all of the time, and then the rest of the day, the collar is taken off.

If you are worried about using it in the wrong manner, you plan to leave it on all day, you don't have any other training methods set up to work with the dog on, or you plan to turn up the frequency too high, then this is a sign that the e collar is not the right option for you. There are a lot of other training methods you can use as well, but for some dog owners, this is the best and most effective one, especially when it comes to dealing with some unwanted behavior that the dog is just not willing to give up. When it is used responsibly, it will help your dog to learn the behaviors you want and can make the training process that much easier.

Types of Devices You Can Use

The good news here is that you can pick from a few different devices that you would like to work with. Each of these will work in a different manner based on what your goals are, and what the dog needs to work on. Let's take a look at the three most common methods that you are able to use, and the three device types that will work the best for most dogs.

First, we have the pet containment system. This is the most common type of the e collar. The point of these containment systems is that it will help to keep your dog inside a space of the home without needing to have a physical barrier. If you want to make sure that while you are gone, the dog stays in one area, then you could set up that parameter so that they don't end up leaving it.

These can even be used outside of the home, such as in the backyard. For some areas where it is hard to make a physical fence, or you don't have the money to put one up, you can use this collar to make sure that the dog will stay in the back and not try to run off from you. You get to choose the area where you would like the puppy to stay while they are wearing the collar.

There are a few different options that you can go with. You can choose a more in-ground installation. Lots of owners who are making an outside fence with the use of the collar will like this method because it will help to keep the lawn looking nice even though there isn't a fence or anything in place. You can do an above-ground installation of the collar to help reinforce a barrier that is already there but still isn't enough to keep the dog contained. And then, if you want to work with this collar to restrict where the dog is able to go into the house, you can use a system that is wireless.

For the most part, the pet containment system is going to work when you are able to install a wire around the perimeter of the yard. This wire is perfectly safe because it is not going to have any current. This is a nice change to another option of the electric fence. These fences are going to carry a current that is at a high voltage that can easily get too strong for your dog. Instead, the wire for the collar is going to form up a closed-loop with a circuit box that can then transmit out a radio signal to the receiver.

This receiver is going to be on the collar that you put on your dog. Then, once you get it all set up, the dog is going to notice and feel that the collar will activate any time they get close to the perimeter that you set. If they stay away from it, then they won't feel anything from the collar at all.

The next type of e collar that your dog can have based on your needs is a bark collar. These are often used by dog owners in order to curb nuisance or excessive barking. When the dog starts to bark, when you have the collar on, they will get a little shock right away. These can be activated with the use of a vibration or a microphone, and some of the collars that you can go with are going to use both the vibration and the sound to help make sure that any noises around the dog are not causing the collar to go off.

And the third option that you can choose when you are picking out an e collar is going to be a training collar or a remote trainer. Training collars of this kind are going to be activated with the help of a device that you can hold onto. Better quality remote trainers are going to have a lot of functions and levels that you can pick with. This helps you to decide how long the stimulation should go on, the quality of the stimulation, and you can even add in some vibration and a beep to the stimulation to make sure you get the attention of the dog ahead of time.

This one is nice because it gives you the full power that you need to take care of your dog properly. You can pick the one that your puppy is most likely to need based on what problem you would like to see fixed. If you have a dog that likes to bark often, then the bark collar would be the best. If you want to use the collar to help with various training techniques and with the training commands, then the training collar is the best. Or, if you just want to make sure that the puppy stays in a specific part of the home or stays in your yard, then the pet containment system is going to be the best for your needs.

Technical Considerations

Understanding how the collar is going to work can make a big difference in the amount of success that you are able to get when you use this collar. It can also help you to understand that your dog is going to be just fine when you use the collar, as long as you decide to use it in a responsible and caring manner. When it is used as a gentle way to train your dog, rather than as a punishment, it is going to be a great tool to include in your arsenal.

The electric shock is going to be characterized on this collar in terms of voltage, current, frequency of the waveform, waveform, pulse rate, and duration. Although the duration of the shock, the current, and the voltage can come together to calculate the amount of energy that is applied, they are not going to be the best indicators to how intense the stimulus is or how the recipient, in this case, the dog, is going to perceive it.

Often, we don't realize how strong something is going to be. A static electric shock, for example, is going to be around 20,000 to 25,000 volts. We have this just by bumping into someone, and it is not going to be painful or damaging to us in any way physically because the current on them is so low. This is the same kind of idea that comes with these collars. The current is going to be so low that your dog is just going to notice it, but won't be hurt.

Depending on the way that the collar is designed, the collar may be set in a way so that the shock given to your dog is just a bit uncomfortable, and nothing more. Variable settings on the collar will be important so that you can adjust the levels to what the dog needs, and you can change it as they grow up as well and need more.

In some cases, these collars are going to be referred to as delivering more of a static shock. The thing to remember here, though, is that the static electricity is going to be a direct current, and it will carry little energy. These collars are going to work more on alternating current ideas. This is why it is not really accurate to refer to the e collars as delivering just a static shock to the dog.

To make sure that there is a consistent stimulation when you want it, you need to make sure that good contact is made between the electrodes on the collar and the skin of your dog. The manufacturer is going to send some instructions on how to fit the collar correctly on your dog to ensure that it fits, and they are not getting harmed in the process. Local humidity and the coat density of the dog, the surface conductivity, and the skin thickness will all come into play as well.

To make this work the best, you will need to experiment a bit and see what is going to work with your dog. Always try it on yourself first to make sure that it is not too strong. But you may start out with a low pulse and find that it does not work with your dog and will slowly increase it from there. Then there are some dogs who can take a lower pulse and be just fine as well. It all depends on your dog, how big they are, and how they respond to the stimulus.

Things to Consider When Using the Collar

Before you decide to go with this kind of collar to help you with training, you need to take a few things into consideration. This is not meant to be a training tool that is going to cause pain or be a punishment for the dog. It is not meant for you to just sit back and do none of the training yourself. And it should not be the only training method that you are going to use.

If you plan to cause pain and use the electronic collar as a form of punishment, then it is probably best to not get a dog at all. This is one of the main reasons that many dog owners are against using this kind of collar in the first place. They don't want to find out that a dog is getting harmed in the process because of a negligent owner.

In addition, the collar is used as another source to train the dog, not as a source of punishment. If you are running inside to grab the collar each time the dog decides to not listen to you, then you need to reconsider using it at all. Bringing it into the training sessions is not a bad thing. But it should be part of the training, and not used to punish the dog during the learning process.

You should also not use this as a lazy way to train your dog. It is fine if it is used to help you speed up the process, such as being worried about the puppy running out of your yard to a busy street or to stop barking when you are already in trouble for it. But you also need to be involved in the training. Working with the dog to show them where their boundaries are, and training them some of the basic commands will make a world of difference in how well they listen to and communicate with you, and can make it so that the collar is barely something that you need.

Along the same lines, the e collar should never be the only training method that you decide to use. It may seem like an easy way to do it, but you need to also form a good bond with your dog, and show them the right way to behave, whether they have the collar on or not. The collar is a great tool, but it should not be on all of the time, and you should not rely on it too much.

A good way to make sure that you don't become too reliant on the collar is to pick out certain times each day when you are allowed to use it, and that is the only time. Maybe you want to make sure the dog stays within a certain confine in the backyard, or you want to stop barking. Then the collar would only be on when they are outside, and the rest of the time, you resort to using other training methods instead.

What to Look for in These Collars

The next thing that you may want to consider when you decide the electronic

collar is the right choice for you is what you need to look for when you want to

pick out the right one. Having a good idea of what you should look for in a shock

collar is going to be important in picking out the one that works for you and your

dog. Just like with any other product that you look for, there are going to be a

high and a low end in the products, and the price is not always going to be the

same as quality.

Most of the time, these collars are going to cost a good amount of money, which means that most owners want to make sure that they are picking out a unit that is higher in quality, that works, and that has a lot of options that go with it. For example, there are a lot of units that are low to mid-range that may work well, but then the battery will die out on them after just a few months, and you either have to go without the collar for some time, or you will have to go and spend a lot of money again.

If you don't already know someone who has one of these collars for their dog that you can ask about, then it is time to find some reviews done on the different products and use those to help you out. Sites like Amazon have a long list of training collars that you are able to take a look at. Pay attention to the good and the bad about the product and decide if this is something that you would like to get or not.

There are a few things that you want to look for when picking out a dog shock collar. You want one that is made well and is not going to fall apart when your dog runs and jumps around. You want to find one that is waterproof because you never know when the dog is going to jump into some water or be outside when a sudden downpour happens. And you want to check out the battery and make sure that it is not going to go bad on you too quickly.

Tips on Using These Collars on Your Dog

As a dog owner, you may know that the training process is going to take some time, and it won't always be as easy as you may think in the beginning. And you may know that the e collar is going to be the best option to help you get the training done faster and more efficiently. But you may be at a loss for how you are able to get the collar to work, and some of the best practices for using this with your dog. Some of the tips that you are able to use in order to get the most out of training your dog how to behave with these e collars will include some of the following:

1. These training collars are meant to be an aid for training. You should use commands that are consistent before you use the button to send the shock. Teach the dog how to follow the commands and give them time to learn, rather than just getting trigger happy and pushing down on it all of the time.

2. The settings, in the beginning, need to be low. Start out with one of the lowest settings and see whether or not the dog responds. You can then go up slowly until the dog starts to respond a bit.

    a. You don't want them to yelp or cry in pain. But a little notice of the shock, like looking up at you or looking around to figure out what is going on, is just fine. With a bit of experimenting, you will find what will work the best for them and what doesn't hurt them.

3. After your dog has gone through a few of the shocks to get the feeling of them, you can use the vibration in place as a type of warning. This is a good reminder for the dog about what is going to come next if they decide not to listen. Over time, your training may only use the vibration rather than the shock at all.

4. Use the bad beep before you give any of the shocks. This is something that the dog is able to catch on to, and they will soon respond to the sound.

5. Use the good sound, or learn how to praise your dog, any time that they respond to the sound in the manner that you would like.

6. If you are training for the dog to stay in your yard, you should consider doing a bit of pre-training before you bring in the shock here.

7. To make sure that the battery lasts as long as possible, you want to do some charging on a frequent basis and do not let the battery stay in the charging position for days at a time, or you will end up ruining the battery in no time.

The Advantages of Using the Shock Collar

There are a lot of people who worry about using this kind of collar on their dog. They feel like it is going to cause a lot of damage to their dog, or that it could turn them very aggressive. The truth is, these can potentially happen, but that is if you don't use the collar in the right manner. If you set it up too high, use the collar too much, or don't teach the dog that their behavior is the reason the collar is going off, then it could potentially cause problems.

There are things that you can do to use the collar in a responsible way. for example, trying the collar on your arm or wrist first to see how strong the shock is before putting it on your dog can help you see how strong it is. Your goal with this is not to make the dog get hurt or be in pain in the process. It is all about showing them how to behave, and a little annoyance from the collar can help make this happen.

There are a few advantages that come with using this kind of collar in order to help you train your dog. First, this kind of collar is going to be effective when you are trying to send your dog a signal if you are far away. You can adjust the amount of current that is used, and you can use just a beeping sound to train your dog to behave to that without even needing to shock the dog. You may need to do the shocks in the beginning along with the beeps. Then, over time you can take the shocks away, and the beeping will be enough to get the dog to behave for you.

These collars are a good way to train your dog on how to listen. Some training needs to be done right away, such as when your dog chooses to bark nonstop when they are outside. This can also be effective at keeping your dog safe if they tend to like to run away from you when you go outside, or they like to explore in areas where they should not be. Training them with the collar will ensure that even a difficult dog will start to listen to you, but you most always use this in a responsible manner.

There are some disadvantages to using this kind of collar, though. First, they can be expensive, and you have to decide if this expense is worth it for you or if you would rather use some of the other training methods. If you are not careful with some of the settings that come with this kind of collar, it is possible that they are going to be too harsh. And some dogs respond well to praise and treats and won't really need to have this kind of collar at all. This is why it is so important to learn the temperament of your dog in particular and keep that in mind when deciding if you need one of these or not.

Remember that when you do buy an e collar, you should also get a collar that can be used on a regular occurrence. Your electronic collar is not something that the puppy should be told to wear all of the time. it is a training tool, and this means that the puppy should be allowed to have some breaks from the collar, rather than having to wear it all of the time.

Picking out an e collar and deciding to use it for your needs can be a big decision. It helps you to work on some of the training that is needed with your dog, even though there are a lot of people who feel that this is really not something that is necessary to do with the dog at all. You have to determine your own training needs, and combine it with the way that your dog is responding to other training methods, the safety of your dog (even if it is only the safety in certain areas where you would use the collar) and how fast you need to work on solving the behavioral problem.

By learning how to use the electronic collar in the proper manner, and ensuring that you are going to try it out first, use it along with other training methods rather than all on its own, and paying attention to how much you actually use this collar, you will be able to find one that works for your dog, and soon they will be trained to listen to your commands and do what you would like.

Chapter 2: Things to Know Before Purchasing an E Collar

Before you run out and decide to purchase one of these e collars, it is important to understand how these e collars work and some of the benefits and negatives that come with using these. You also want to make sure that you understand what to look for when you pick out these collars and some of the benefits that come with it. Some of the things to remember when you decide to go with one of these e collars include:

You Can Adjust the Intensity

One of the neat things that come with these kinds of collars is that you are able to adjust the amount of intensity that comes with them. You can even choose to work with the vibration mode or a warning beep rather than just the shock level. And the level of the shock can be adjusted based on what works for you and for your dog.

For those who are worried about using the shock collar because they think it is going to harm their dog, knowing that you can have a lot of control, and use different modes, can be really comforting and nice. Other collars, including the spray collars that administer a harmless but foul-smelling blast up the nose of your dog, are not going to be adjustable, which gives this kind of collar a leg up on the competition.

Fast results

Many dog owners like to go with this kind of collar because it helps them to get some fast results to help with training. In fact, when it is used in the proper manner, it only takes a few shocks in order to correct most of the unwanted behavior that happens in your dog. And once those few shocks are done; you will be able to use the warning vibration was enough to get the dog to behave in the manner that you want.

This is great news. After a few little shocks that are more uncomfortable rather than anything else, you will be able to rely just on the vibration or the beep that comes with the collar. This helps to keep the dog safe and will make it easier to get the results that you want without having to shock your dog all of the time. Some dogs are a bit more stubborn with this, and you may need to shock them a few more times, but you will be pleasantly surprised at how little you will need to get the dog to listen and how quickly you can stop using the shocks.

You Don't Have to be Nearby All the Time

Shock collars, when you use them properly to control barking that is chronic, can even be used when you are not out with the dog, say when you are gone for work for the day. this can be helpful when you need to leave the dog outside while you are gone, and the neighbors complain about the barking. The same goes when you use the shock collar to help with controlling boundaries, though you do need to be there in the beginning to do hands-on training with the dog.

Now, there are some people who would not want to leave their dog on the collar unattended because this means that overcorrecting can occur, and you are not there to observe and adjust the situation as needed. But the choice is yours, and most dogs are going to be just fine being on the collar without any help from the owners.

They are Affordable

When you are debating whether to get a shock collar or not as a training device, when you compare it to getting a fence or a professional dog trainer, you will find that the collar is going to be a lot less expensive. Most of the time, these are going to be around $250 for the higher-end models, but you can find them for a bit cheaper.

You will want to determine the features that you are able to find when you work with this kind of product. Some may give you control over the collar with a remote, some allow you to adjust the warning and the shock levels, some will give you a range of distances that the dog can go through, and some even have more than one collar available at a time.

Check through all of the specifications that come with these kinds of collars ahead of time. this will ensure that you are not picking out something that is not going to work or may cause pain to the dog without you knowing what is going on.

The Negatives that Come with the Shock Collars

Before we move on from all of this positive and all of the good things that we are able to get from the shock collars, it is important to see some of the drawbacks and why some people are so against using these collars in the first place. Remember, though, that while these may be valid complaints for some, often a good dog owner, someone who is using it as a tool and will use other positive reinforcement along the way, will not experience any issues with this kind of collar at all.

The first issue that can sneak in is that owners are worried about the shock. Many times, the dog owner doesn't want to cause any pain to their own pet. Keep in mind that these collars are going to allow you to control the amount of intensity that you give to the dog with this shock, but you are still going to give them a little shock that can be uncomfortable for the dog.

Another issue is that the collar could end up causing fear to some dogs. Fear in any animal, especially a dog, is going to be dangerous, so you have to make sure that you are using the collar as a training method that doesn't rely on fear. If the collar is not used in the proper manner, it could cause the dog to learn how to fear situations, objects, and even people that they may associate back with the collar.

You may find that a problem is going to occur with overcorrection sometimes. Without you actually there to watch the e collar, and when you can't watch the shock that is given out, there is a chance that the electric fence and the automatic bark collars are going to deliver shocks too often, or when they are not even needed. This is going to confuse the dog, or it could correct a problem that isn't even there to start with.

And the big reason that a lot of people are worried about working with this kind of collar is that they worry that it doesn't provide the dog with any positive reward, which means that the good behavior of the dog is not being reinforced when you use the collar.

Positive reinforcement is going to include things like a treat, verbal approval and praise, and your attention. So while this kind of collar can be effective at deterring some of the negative behaviors that you want to avoid, like barking all of the time, there is an issue with it not helping you to reward and promote some of the positive behaviors that you want them to keep on doing. This is why with any kind of training program, you want to make sure that there is some positive reinforcement.

This problem is easily fixed if you choose to use the e collar just as a training tool, rather than using it for all of the training. This allows you to still find plenty of other opportunities during the day to reward the positive behavior while using the collar to avoid some of the negative behaviors that you are not fond of the dog using. Putting these all together can make a difference in how well the dog will behave and can ensure that your dog knows how to do what you want, no matter what you are training them on.

There are a lot of good benefits that come with using this kind of collar to help you to train your dog and get them ready to exhibit the behaviors that you want them too. But it is most important for you to be present when the collar is being used. This will ensure that the dog is only getting the shock when they need it, and can prevent issues with the dog not getting a positive reward or the shock going off at the wrong times and the dog not learning the behavior that you want them to.

Learning how to use the collar as a way to train your dog, and figuring out the schedule that works the best for you both so that the dog can actually learn the behaviors that you want them to is going to be critical here. It will help you to watch that the problems are improving, and to be on top of anything that may go wrong with the collar.

Chapter 3: The Accessories You Need

One thing that you need to consider when picking out your e collar is what kind

of accessories you will need. Most reputable companies are going to give you a

battery with the collar that is long-lasting and that you are able to recharge with

relative ease. If this is not offered with the collar, then you need to make sure that

you are purchasing a battery so that you can actually use the collar the way that

you want. You can also choose from a few different styles of collars that you

would like to work with. And one of the most important things with this is that

you will have some access to a variety of contact points based on the one you

choose to go with.

So, to start with purchasing one of these collars that comes with batteries, you can recharge is critical. There are some options that are lower in price, but the battery is not rechargeable, and you will find that you are replacing the batteries more often than you want. And when you have to replace them all the time, there is a bigger pain because they are special ones that aren't easy to find at your local stores. Yes, the units with the rechargeable battery may be more expensive, but in the long run, getting this kind is going to really save you. A good quality collar of this kind will have rechargeable batteries in the collar as well as these in the remote.

Another upgrade that you may want to consider working with is a bungee collar. There is an attachment like this that can work for the majority of e collars and are able to help these stretch out to the size that your dog will need. You will find that all of the e collars are either going to have a collar that is one inch or .75-inch-wide, so it is easy to find these bungee collars for any of the electronic collars you choose to purchase.

This is such a great thing to do. While you will see how to fit the collar on your dog in the next chapter, it is possible that your dog's neck will go up in size a bit when they are running around, and their temperature rises. The bungee collar is a good addition to deal with this so that the collar is not too small when they are running around and not too big when they are resting.

You should also consider having a collar that has a few contact points for your dog because this is essential to having the most consistent training with this kind of collar. It is easy to feel like your dog has a high pain threshold, and that is why they are not feeling anything that you do with the collar. This is not the case, and often the problem is going to lay with the contact points that you have in the collar you purchased.

Often, it is easy to solve this kind of problem if you have a collar that can change up the contact point based on whether your dog has a coat that is short, medium, long, or extra thick. With short to medium-haired dog, you are going to be fine with a contact point that is already in the e collar when you purchase it. But what works for these dogs will not work as well with those that have long or thick coats because they just won't be able to feel it.

The short points of contact can be a great option to work with if you have a dog that includes Great Danes, Boxers, English Bulldogs, French Bulldogs, Bull Terriers, and all of the bully breed dogs. The medium contact point is going to work the best for options like Border Collies, Labrador Retrievers, and Goldendoodles. The longer contact points will work with some dogs like German shepherds, golden retrievers, and Rottweilers.

Then if you are working with some of the dogs that have a really thick coat such as Akitas, Great Pyrenees, and the Bernese Mountain Dogs, then you will want to go with the thick coat contact. And finally, an extra long contact point is going to work for dogs like the Newfoundland.

You have to take a look at the kind of dog you are working with and then go from there to figure out which kind of contact point is going to be the best. You do not want to go with the long contact point on a dog breed that is a bit smaller and who doesn't have a lot of hair because this is going to be too much for them and can cause pain. But if you have a dog that has more hair or is bigger, the longer points are better to make sure that they will even feel the shock collar when it is in use.

In addition, most of the contact points that are found with these collars are going to be made out of surgical grade stainless steel. The reason that this is used is that this kind of material is not going to rust or corrode away, even if your dog is in a saltwater kind of condition. Make sure that you pick out a collar that meets with this because it will ensure that you are going to be able to use the device for some time.

If you put the electronic collar on your dog and you notice that the neck of the dog seems to be irritated, go through and double-check that the contact points from the collar are stainless steel. If these points are made out of this material, and you notice that the irritation is still there, you can get a contact point that is hypoallergenic and made out of titanium.

The issue of your dog's neck getting annoyed with the contact points is going to be rare, but there are some dogs that are going to be slightly allergic to the small amount of nickel that is found inside of the stainless steel with these contact points, so if they do get irritated, then you just need to pick out a covering that will help to make their skin not come in contact with the stainless steel, and the nickel that it contains at all.

Picking out the e collar that is going to work for your dog requires you to have a good understanding of your dog and how they are going to respond to it. You need to be prepared to spend a bit more, because this will ensure that you get a collar that is actually going to work, one that is going to not cause any issues with your dog, and one that will be a great addition to the training regimen that you do while allowing the dog to actually feel the shock or the vibration from the collar. Following some of the tips in this chapter, and double-checking that the collar has the right accessories can make things so much easier.

Chapter 4: Properly Fitting the Collar on Your Dog

The next thing that we need to take a look at is the idea of getting the collar to fit your dog just right. You don't want to let the collar get too tight, or the current from the shock will be too much, and the contact points are going to rub and irritate the dog. But if you end up not getting the collar tight enough, then it is not going to phase the dog at all when they do something that sets it off. This is a careful balance that you need to work on to ensure that your dog is going to be comfortable, while also making sure that they are going to be able to feel the training method that you use.

The two most common mistakes that a dog owner can make when they get started with this kind of training is that they don't use the right contact points for the collar, and they don't end up fitting the collar onto their dog in the proper manner. The stimulation that the e collar is going to deliver is going to be similar and will feel in a similar manner, as chiropractors like to use for muscle rehabilitation. This means that if the collar is not reaching the right kind of contact with the muscles of the dog, then the stimulation that they experience will be inconsistent.

Another common mistake that some pet owners are going to do is that they put the collar down, so it is too low on the neck of the dog. This is not a good idea because of the shape of your dog's neck. The dog is going to be bigger at the base of their neck, or lower down, compared to at the top of the neck. So, if you end up placing this collar, so it is at the base of the neck when your dog is outside playing around outside, the collar will go up the neck and will lose the snug fit that it had at the start.

The good news is that many of the collars out there are going to tell you what kind of dog breed you are able to put the collar on, so you can get a good idea of whether this is going to work for your dog or not. Always look at the description or ask the company directly to figure out if a particular collar is big enough or small enough for your dog.

Once the collar gets to your home, there is going to be a bit of adjusting that you can do with the collar. This is when you will use the two-finger rule to make sure that the collar fits your dog properly. Most collars are going to have some kind of range of the types of dogs it will fit, so you will have to figure out how to use this and to get the electronic collar to fit well on your dog so that it works in the proper manner.

So, get the collar up on the neck in the right position, and then tighten it up to where you think it needs to go. Then, slide two fingers in and see if it is going to fit or not. If you can fit more than two fingers in there, then the collar is too loose, and you need to tighten it a bit more. If you can't get the two fingers in there and barely one fits, then it is time to loosen it up so that it doesn't cause discomfort to the dog.

A good place to help you with referencing where to place this is to cinch the collar down so that you are able to slip in two of your fingers underneath the collar strap on the back of the neck of your dog. Some of the steps that you can follow to make sure that you get this kind of collar to fit on your dog in the proper manner will include the following:

1. Make sure that before you put the collar on at all that the right contact points are already present. For example, if your dog is allergic to nickel and you know this ahead of time, make sure that the right attachments are placed on it before using.

2. De-shed the neck of the dog if they happen to have a coat that is a bit thicker.

3. Place the collar so that it ends up higher on the neck of your dog.

4. Do not place on the top of the neck of your dog. You can pick either the right or the left sides of the dog are fine.

5. Tighten the collar so that it is to a snug fit on the dog. You can tell that it is a snug fit when you can fit two fingers under the collar. This makes sure that it is close enough that your dog will be able to feel it, but loose enough that it isn't causing irritation and pain to the dog.

6. Be sure that if the dog is wearing this collar for a long period of time, you should rotate it around every two hours or more. This makes sure that no irritation shows up with the collar.

7. It is often recommended that when the e collar is on, you should not attach a leash to the dog either.

As we just mentioned, it is best if you do not attach the leash to the dog when they have this collar on. The Martingale collar can be a great option to use during training and they are inexpensive while being easy to find at any pet store in your area. Any harness or collar that you want to use to attach your leash is just fine. Your goal here is to make sure that they are the right size for the kind of dog you have, and that they can be fitted tightly to the neck of the dog.

The martingale collar is going to end up tightening if the dog tries to back out of the collar, which is why a lot of dog trainers like to work with it to get the dog to behave the way that they should. If your dog is able to back their way out of the collar, then the martingale collar is the best option to eliminate the chance of this happening when you are trying to train the puppy on how to behave with the collar.

With that said, it is best if you are able to either slip the e collar off your dog before you use the leash or put on the harness or another type of collar and then hook up the leash to that one. Hooking the leash so that it is on the e collar is just going to cause problems. The dog could get out of it, the movements they do while on the leash may make the collar go off without any need to, and it could make things more difficult when you are doing the training process with your dog.

It is much better to work with the e collar as a training tool, and then when you are ready to go on a walk with the dog, or you want to work on some other form of training, take the collar off. It is best to not leave this kind of collar on more than you need. This helps the dog to get a break from using this kind of collar and ensures that you are not leaving it on for too long.

Remember that the collar is just meant to be a training tool and not something that your dog wears all of the time. And once they get more adjusted to the collar and stop doing the behavior that you got the collar for in the first place, then it may be time to stop using the collar any longer.

The final thing that we need to take a look at here is the idea of safety. Your goal here is to use the collar as a way to safely and effectively train your dog to behave the way that you want, not to harm them or cause them any kind of pain. Following the right safety procedures will ensure that you can meet both of these goals in no time.

If you ever have it where the dog is going to need to keep the collar on for more than a few hours at a time, make sure that you do some rotating of the collar after a few hours. So, if the collar is on for eight hours, you will need to move it around three or four times. Moving it from left to right or from right to left is just fine for this process.

You may find that some dogs are going to be able to wear the collar in the same spot for a longer period of time, and other dogs will need to change the position around the neck on a more frequent basis. You have to learn what seems to work the best for your dog, but starting out with a rotation after two hours of the collar is a good place for you to start, and helps you to at least move the collar a few times throughout the day.

Also, if your dog is going to swim anywhere, then it is usually a good thing for you to take the collar off them completely. This allows them to get a break and ensures that the collar will be fine. Most of these collars are going to be waterproof, so if they jump into a pool or something without you being able to catch them, the collar will be fine. But it is best if you are able to take it off and give the dog a break, and then allow the neck of the dog to dry off all the way before you try to put the collar back on.

Any time that you need to wash the e collar, make sure to use some warm and soapy water. You should try to wash this on a bi-weekly or so basis to make sure that nothing gets on the collar and causes issues. If it needs to be done more often because your dog likes to make some messes, then this is fine as well. Give the collar some time to dry off after the cleaning before putting it back on the neck of your dog.

Making sure that the collar is going to fit your dog properly, and that you will be able to get it to work on them, without causing any irritation or other issues, is something that takes a bit of practice and some knowledge about your dog. But once you are able to pick out the right kind and get it fitted in the right manner, you are going to see how great this training tool can be to help your dog learn the behaviors they are allowed to use, and the ones that you want them to stop doing now.

Chapter 5: Off-Leash Training with the E Collar

Now that we have the right collar for your dog and you have had some time to try it on and get it nice and fitted, it is time to work on a bit of off-leash training with your puppy. Before we decide to transition off the leash with the dog, there are four major pillars that all dog owners need to know to make this process a bit easier, including:

1. Where the stimulation is going to come from.

2. How to turn the stimulation on.

3. How to turn the stimulation off

4. How to avoid stimulation in the first place.

It is common for a lot of dog owners, who may be well-meaning, to rush the training process with the e collar, without taking the time to properly train their dog without the collar. Rushing this process often seems like the best option, and whether you are excited to try out some new training with your dog or you just want to get the process done, it is going to be a bad decision for both your dog and for you in the long term.

When an owner decides to rush the process, they are almost always going to be really frustrated with the dog, and they decide that training the dog has to be done now, whether or not the dog is ready for it or not. It is tempting to skip a few steps along the way, but let's follow all of these steps so that you can do right by your dog. And always remember that the training we will do is not just for the dog, but also for you as the dog owner.

Let's stay with the first three days of training. During this time, your goal is to just do two quick sessions a day. you can do one in the morning and one in the evening inside of your apartment or home. And keep the training sessions pretty short. Five minutes up to ten at the most, depending on how your dog is responding to the training. Some people find that their dog is motivated by food so doing the training for a few minutes before feeding them can help you out with the training.

If you decide that this is the method to use, you can give your dog a small amount of food for each repetition during the training session until the meal is all done. Other times using the treats can be a good motivation as well. You can pick any treat that you want, as long as it is a favorite of your dog, so they will be motivated to listen and do what you want.

First, we need to stop and determine which method you would like to use in order to get the attention of the dog with the e collar, the tone, or the vibration. When we start to progress off-leash and work at long distances, this step will prove to be of benefit and will be paired together with the recall command of "come."

This method of prompting is going to depend on the model of the collar that you use and the company that makes it. If you have a collar that is able to give an audible tone, you will need to use the tone. If the collar has a vibration, then we need to use that. Then there are some collars that will offer you both options and if this is the case, working with the tone is the best because some dogs are going to start feeling scared of the vibrate setting, and this is going to slow down the progress that you are making with the process.

The next thing to work on here is to train on the e collar and the remote and then making sure that you are able to get the collar to fit in the proper manner around your dog's neck. You will begin with the session inside of your house, using a regular six to eight-foot leash on the dog. Tell them to come and then tap the T/V button as you walk away from the dog. Say Yes and then give the dog some food or a treat and some praise for doing what you say for coming to you.

If this is working the way that it should and the dog is paying attention to the command that you are giving, then you will notice that the dog will start to follow you around the room. You can also try out with a few other commands, but remember that this session for the first few days should only last for a few minutes, five tops, so you will need to end it pretty quickly.

When the training session is done, make sure that the dog gets a lot of praise and attention. Praise them when they come to you and for doing so well with following you around or doing any other command that you would like to use. This may seem a bit silly, but the more praise that you give, and the bigger deal that you give for the work, the more that the dog will associate the T/V with something that brings them lots of good things.

It is important for you to only work with the e collar for these first lessons for days one to three. Then we will move on to the second part. For days four to seven, you are going to stick with the two sessions per day for a bit longer. These lessons, though, are going to move from the inside to the outside, often in the yard or when you take the dog on a leash walk. Keep the sessions pretty short, not going more than seven minutes for this one.

What we are going to work with over these days is going to help cover many of the teaching points that will help to prepare your dog for the off-leash control that you want to have later on. It is also going to make sure that your dog is going to know the four pillars of e collar training that we talked about before so that they will listen to what you have to say.

Every time that you get started on a new lesson, you should start out by finding the e collar working level for your dog. This has to be done each time, even if it is on the same day, to make sure that the level is never too high or too low for your dog. Think of the working level as the lowest point that your dog is going to feel while still showing you a slight response that they feel this stimulation. It is nowhere near strong enough for them to feel pain or get harmed, but it is definitely strong enough to get their attention.

So, how do we make sure that we are able to find this working level? A good place to start is to practice finding your own working level. Place the collar so that it is on your hand and start the stimulation at the first level. Then give the button a tap. Then go up one level at a time until you start to feel a bit of tingling in your hand. This is going to be the working level of the e collar for you. You now have to figure out when this is happening for your dog, and it is most likely going to be at a different level than what you feel. Make sure that your sessions always start out by finding this level to make things a bit easier and to ensure the training session will be successful.

How to Find the Initial Level

There are a lot of behaviors that your dog is going to show when they are wearing this collar, and they start to feel some of the stimulation. The most common response that you are going to see is your dog looking around them like there is a bug that has landed on their neck or on their head. There are some dogs that may just stop what they are doing right now and look confused. And some dogs will not really show a change other than a bit of muscle twitching on their neck (this is the most common with the bully breeds). Another sign of this is that the dog is going to lick their lips or do other subtle signs along the way.

Each dog is going to respond to the whole e collar thing in a different manner, and it is your job to figure out the best way that your dog is going to respond. Starting at the lowest level and moving up slowly, watching for any kind of sign can be another way to make sure that you pick out the right kind of stimulation that works for your dog.

You can start out with a level on the collar that is 1/100, and then tap the continuous button once quickly and then watch for a slight change to show up in the behavior of your dog. Continue going up to two, and then three, and so on until you start to see a sign from your dog, including some that we talked about above. When you find this level, then you know that this is the perfect level to start the lesson.

With this, you need to restart the process each time. This makes it easier for you to find the level that is perfect for your dog, no matter what time of day or even what day it is. And always slowly build up from the bottom. It is easy to assume that your dog is not going to be able to feel the lower levels of the stimulation, but there are some dogs that are going to feel it at really low levels, and making sure that they aren't getting harmed by starting way up at the highest points can be critical to your success with this.

Now that you know the right stimulation levels for your dog, it is time to start with some of the training sessions for these second set of days. Start by walking your dog in the yard, or even on the sidewalk that is right in front of your home.

Once you see that the dog starts to fixate on something that is in front of you, and they start to get close to pulling on the leash, you can stop, say come, and then tap the T/V button. If the dog looks a bit confused, you want to encourage them to walk to you and walk away while enticing them with a treat. Be sure that you offer some praise and a treat of some kind when they do end up coming to you.

It is possible that the dog is going to become too distracted by the smells and the sights of the outdoors, and you may need to move on to the continuous stimulation button at the level that works on the e collar for your dog. This may get their attention a bit more so that they will decide to listen to you rather than going after the object that has gotten their attention.

As you progress in the training lessons, you may find that you will need to slightly increase the level of stimulation on the collar. This is common as the dog gets more used to the feeling and decides that they are able to ignore it and not listen to what you want them to do. Never jump up more than one level at a time when you are doing this because it could harm the dog, and you often need a lower level than you think.

Once we are to this point, it is time to move on to the training that is needed for days seven to twelve. You are going to work on pretty much the same ideas that we focused on in the last section, but your recalls are going to become increasingly difficult by incrementally adding in more distraction and distance. You will use a long leash for this one, and if you are able to find one that goes up to fifteen or more feet, this can make the process a bit easier. Remember that your end goal here is to take the dog off the leash, so you need them to pass a few tests before you are able to do this.

With these sessions, you need to get the work done outside. You can then increase the session a bit longer here, and instead of just focusing on the five minutes, you can increase up to thirty minutes to make sure that the new skills that you are teaching to the dog will stick. Two sessions a day is going to work with this as well.

Before you get started with this kind of training, make sure that the collar fits the dog well. Then turn it on, attach the long leash, and make sure you have lots of food and treats ready to help. Start your dog out with an easy lesson by putting something that your dog is going to like in the yard before you even take the dog outside. Plant four or five of these in different areas and then take the dog out for a walk, allowing them to smell around but don't allow them enough room to go and get them.

Find the right level on the collar for the dog and then tell them to "come' when they start to go towards the hot dog and tap on the T/V button. If you find that the dog isn't coming right to you, then hold down on the continuous button for one to two seconds, and start walking in the other direction. If your dog does come to you, even if it took a few seconds, make sure to give them lots of praise and a treat for listening.

Because the distraction is pretty strong in this one, you may have to work for a

bit. If the dog decides to ignore the first-come command and the T/V and then

they also decide to ignore the continuous button, it is time to slowly increase the

level of the e collar until they avoid the hot dogs and decide to start walking along

with you. Once they do this, you can shower them with praise and give them the treats or the food that you brought with you. Then move on to the next hot dog distraction and continue on with the same thing until all of it is done or 30 minutes have passed. You will find that your dog will quickly learn that they can avoid the stimulation that you send over just by focusing on you and coming when they hear the tone or feel the vibration.

The most important thing to remember here is to give your dog a lot of praise along the way. if the only part of the training that you are doing is the stimulation to get them away from the distraction, the process is going to be slow, and you are not going to get the results that you want. You want to make the dog feel like coming to you and leaving the distraction alone is way more worth it than the distraction. And the best way to do that is to add in the stimulation that they don't want, and a lot of good praise, which they do want.

This positive reinforcement is something that you want to pay attention to with any kind of training that your dog is doing with you. This is basically when you reward the dog for all of the good behavior that they do with praise, treats, and other rewards of your choosing. This helps them to learn quickly what you want them to do, and because they want to please you, they are going to remember those good behaviors and the treats and rewards that they got for them, much faster.

When you are able to couple together the positive reinforcement with the stimulation from the collar, you will find that the dog will quickly learn that going after the distraction on a walk is not worth it. If they just follow you, they can avoid the stimulation, while getting a treat and lots of praise along the way. And for most dogs, this is going to be much more rewarding overall, and they will learn quickly.

Each dog is going to be a bit different. Some will need higher levels of stimulation to get them to listen. Some may take a few weeks to learn how to walk around with you without a leash. And some are going to be more stubborn, and you will just have to add in some more consistency in order to get them to follow along with you. But if you use the right level of stimulation, and you make sure that you add in a ton of positive reinforcement for your dog, they will get them off the leash training down.

And those are the steps that you need to use in order to train your dog to walk off the leash. Over time, you will be able to take the e collar off and still get the dog to listen to you and follow along without any leash, just lots of praise, and maybe a few treats. It does take at least a few weeks to get this down, especially if your dog is prone to following distractions. But it can really make walks more enjoyable and helps to make sure that the dog learns how to listen to you and follow your commands, no matter where you may take them.

Chapter 6: Perimeter Training with the E Collar

Now that we have had some time to look at how to train your dog to follow you without a leash and without running off to any of the distractions that come up along the walk, it is time to work with some perimeter training with the dog. There are a lot of people and dog owners who get this kind of collar to help keep the dog in their back yard, even if there is not a good fence up in place and ready to use. You can let the collar do some of the work on its own, but you need to be present during this training to make sure that the dog will know exactly where they are allowed to be.

Just like with some of the other types of training that you do with this collar, perimeter training needs to be done after you have had a chance to set up the initial foundations of commands and training with your dog. This means that they should know at least a few basic commands so that they know how to behave when you work on this.

There are two options that you are able to work with when it comes to perimeter training. You can do it with the e collar, or you can choose to do it with a perimeter containment system. Both of these work on a similar idea as one another, but you will find that it is going to have a little different setup.

First, let's take a look at the perimeter training when you decide to use the e collar. Some of the strengths that you will find by choosing this option over the other includes:

1. You will not have to purchase any additional systems or items to do this if you already own an e collar for the dog.

2. This gives you the ability to be more subtle with the training if you are using an e collar with 100 levels.

3. You will get the ability to correct some of the dirty thoughts that the dog could be thinking when it comes to challenging the boundary.

4. You get to be in control of quickly stopping the stimulation if the dog challenges the boundary and is confused about what they need to do in order to make it stop.

5. You get the ability to make sure your dog will be perimeter trained on more than one property without having to get a containment system for each one.

There is a weakness with this one. If you use the e collar to train the dog on where they are supposed to stay all of the time, then you will be responsible for watching the dog more during the training period. You will be the one responsible for bringing the stimulation on, and if you are not there, then the dog can just walk over the line without any repercussions and will run off without you.

This is not necessarily a bad thing. The more that you can be involved in any kind of training that you do with your dog, even with this kind of collar, the better it is for everyone involved. You should be present to watch the dog and make sure they learn the boundaries that they can roam in and the e collar kind of forces you to do just that.

The other option that you are able to work with when training your dog how to follow their boundaries is going to be the perimeter containment system. This is a system that is put in place like an electric fence almost and will be set up by you to say how far the dog is able to roam. When the dog gets close to the perimeter, the system is going to start sending out the stimulation to tell the dog to move away. There are a few benefits that come with using this kind of system for perimeter training, including:

1. This one is always going to be consistent because the machine is going to be able to turn the stimulation on and off for your dog each time they get close.
2. It gives you the ability to use more of your property, like the sides of the property that are sometimes a bit harder to self-monitor.

There are some weaknesses that come with using this method, of course. The biggest one is that you will need to get an additional unit set up, and then you need to go through and install it properly. Most perimeter containment systems are not going to provide you with a lot of levels of stimulation that they can promise. Most of these are just going to have between three to six levels, and this makes some of the subtle training that you need a bit harder to do. And if you have more than one property that you want to train the dog on with perimeter training, it is much harder with the containment system.

Now it is time to dive right into some of the steps that you can use with perimeter training. This is going to be day one to three with your dog, and we are going to focus on using the e collar for the best benefits. Your first step with this is to put on the collar and attach it to a standard leash. Find the working level that is the best for your dog, and then begin by walking your dog up to the rope. As you walk past the line, you will find that most dogs are going to try jumping over the rope to continue walking along with you.

If this does happen with your dog, hold down the continuous button, and walk the dog back onto the perimeter and then release the button. You may have to do a few repetitions of this one, but soon the dog is going to catch on. Continue with this ten to fifteen times, without saying anything when the dog passes the line or goes back. We want to get the dog to believe with this one that the stimulation turned on because they passed the line, not because of anything that you are doing.

Using the verbal commands or praise when the dog goes on either side of the line may seem like the best thing to do, but then you are going to bring in a new challenge later on. If you do this, the dog is going to think that you were doing the stimulation. And once you go inside, or the dog thinks that no one is actually watching them, then they are going to challenge the line and could end up running off.

Once you have been able to get your dog to understand the concept, and they won't go past the line even when you do, it is time to move on to the second step for this training. This should be done within a few days, so if your dog is still being stubborn or struggling, go ahead and increase the collar level and then try again. To know that you are ready to move on to the next step, you should be able to walk across the line with your dog, still on the leash, and have them stop at the line every time, without you doing any commands.

At this point, it is time to start taking the dog to other areas of the yard and see if you are able to follow the same process. You can switch over to the long leash, and allow the dog to drag it with them. If you find that the dog tries to follow with you rather than staying in the perimeter, then you need to hold down on the continuous button, then release it once the dog goes back, on their own, behind the line.

During this process, be willing and able to help your dog with the leash if you feel like they are getting confused, but the goal is to get them to do this all on their own, without any commands from you. Do this five to ten times, or until the dog catches on, in all the areas of your yard.

Then we are going to move on to day four to seven of the perimeter training. When we get to this stage, you can try adding in some distractions that could show up on the other side of your boundary line. you may even want to work your way up so that at some point, your dog is going to see other dogs that walk by your property. Start out with a lower working level and then increase as is needed depending on the distraction that you see.

After you get through about three weeks of this, keeping the dog within the perimeter that you set, without any commands and just the stimulation helping out, you will be able to remove the visual boundary if you would like. When you see that the dog is doing a good job with this without much help at all, then take off the long leash and continue to add in more distractions to double-check the reliability of your dog and to make sure that they are not going to run away from you.

This process is one that takes some time. you are trying to teach your dog to stay in the yard, where you are able to see them, despite distractions and an urge to just run free. And you are doing this with a collar, rather than with a physical barrier that is going to stop them. Your dog is going to need a few weeks or more to get accustomed to this process and to learn where their boundaries are. But if

you do this in the right manner, and you learn how to take your time with the

process of training with the e collar, you will find that you can get your dog to stay

in the designated area, no matter where you go, and even with a lot of

distractions and no physical boundaries, like a fence, there to make them stay

put.

Chapter 7: When to Use Commands and When Not to Use Commands

When we get to this part of the training process, you want to make sure that you add in the collar some more so that they can get used to having it on, and so that you are able to begin to stop any bad behaviors that your dog has. This could include things like pulling on the leash, jumping on people, or a lot of excessive barking.

In the beginning, the e collar may be on the dog more than it isn't. As long as you are careful with the levels that you are using it, and you remember to turn the collar around on a regular basis so that it doesn't irritate the skin of your dog, this is going to be fine. And if you are effective with your training methods, you will be able to use the collar for a few weeks or so, and find that your dog will be trained to act the way that you want, with none of the negative behaviors.

Remember back to when we were talking about the four pillars from before. These are so important when it comes to training your dog on the e collar, but now we are going to break from tradition a bit and tell you to slightly break away from these four pillars. Trust that this is going to work at getting us to take the training up to the next level for the best results.

One important thing to remember about training your dog is that all good dog training works when the owner is present, great dog training works even if the owner is not present. There are going to be times when you are not present, and you still want the dog to behave. If you go on vacation and someone stops by to feed and walk the dog, you don't want them to jump all over the person. After perimeter training, there will be times when you want to let the dog outside to play and run around without having to physically be out there with them making sure that they behave.

And that is where we are going to start out with this chapter. Let's unpack some of the commands and behaviors that we want to use vocal commands for. In the last chapter on perimeter training, we talked about how you did not want to use commands. This is due to the fact that you want the dog to follow the boundary, whether you are there or not. But then with off-leash training, we did use a command. Learning when to work with the commands and when they are not necessary can make a difference.

Sometimes, you will use the e collar to help with training, and you will want to use some command to go with it. Commands including drop it, go to bed, down, leave it, heel, and come are going to be used in a way that indicates something that you would like the dog to do. Let's call these commands, to make things a bit easier, action commands. These commands are going to be given in a vocal command because it helps the dog learn what we would like them to do.

Then there is the other side of things. This is going to include the moments where we are not going to give commands like the ones before. These behaviors are going to be known as automatic avoidance behaviors. When a dog commits these behaviors, you will not want to give them any verbal cues, because they already know that when they feel the continuous stimulation that they can stop that feeling by doing the opposite behavior. If you have trained the dog right, a command is not necessary because they will just do the action that stops the stimulation.

When we try to use some commands to help with stopping these behaviors, some dogs are going to try and cheat the system a bit when they notice that you are not around to watch. For example, if you tell your dog not to jump on people when they are at the door, even if you used the e collar to help with this training, it may not work. It is possible that the moment someone walks into the door early when you were not expecting them, the dog is going to jump on them because you were not there to use the command word of NO JUMPING.

Of course, this is not what we want to have happened. You want to make sure that the dog learns that they are not allowed to do some of these behaviors, whether or not you are around to witness them doing these behaviors. And that is why there are some training sessions where you will avoid all commands and only work with the collar instead.

When you train the dog that they are going to feel a shock or the stimulation each time that they jump on someone who comes through the door (or does some other behavior that you don't approve of), without any command, then they are going to learn to stop doing that behavior as quickly as possible. Even when you are not there to stop them, they will know that if they jump on the other person who comes through the door, there is a big possibility that they are going to get the stimulation, and they do not like that.

But they learn it the other way as well. If they get a stimulation when they jump on another person, but they avoid the stimulation by not jumping on the other person, what choice do you think the dog is likely to make? If the e collar training went well, the dog will choose to sit quietly (though they may be wagging their tail excitedly) when someone walks through the door in order to avoid the stimulation.

Using commands when you are trying to stop bad behaviors is not necessarily a bad thing, and it does work. But you will find that the e collar training without the command in most cases is going to be more effective, especially when it comes to times when you just can't be present to stop the negative behavior from happening.

When you are trying to figure out whether you should add in a command or not, figure out whether you want to have the dog stop the behavior when you are there, or if you want to make sure that the dog is always acting in a certain manner, whether you are there or not.

When you take the dog on a walk, and you want to make sure that the dog is going to stay near you and not run away, a command is going to be just fine. You are going to always be there when the dog is walking, so having a command to get their attention and to give them a chance to return back to you before using the stimulation makes sense. Any time that you are working with a command like this, then you can go ahead and come up with a clicker word or another phrase that will tell the dog that it is time to listen to you.

On the other hand, there are some actions that you want to make sure the dog is always following, whether they can see that you are near to them or not. When you are working on perimeter training, and you want the dog to stay in the designated area, or you are working on making sure the dog doesn't jump on others whether you can make it to the front door quickly enough or not, then teaching the dog how to behave with the e collar, and without any command, is going to be better. This teaches the dog that it is the collar that is telling them to stop, rather than the owner, and they will worry about how to behave whether you are near or not.

No matter how much you love your dog, you don't want to spend all day watching them and making sure that they behave. You want to have them behave whether you are around to watch or not. With the right use of the e collar in the training process, you will find that this is easier to do and it won't be long before you are able to get the dog to listen to you and to follow your rules, whether or not you are around to control the behavior.

Chapter 8: Forms of Correction with Your Dog

As you are working with any training method, whether it is with the e collar or some other method, you need to have some idea in place on how you are going to correct the course of your dog, especially when they are really not listening to you. Think of correct as a way for you as the dog owner to correct the course that your dog is on when the dog is about to jump on someone when they are running across the yard to get away, or when they are ignoring some command that you are trying to give.

Corrections can come in a lot of different forms. You will find that these can be verbal in nature, but it is also possible to get them to work more effectively when you pair them with the physical reminder of some kind. This is where the e collar is going to come in. Your collar level for corrections, if you choose to use it in this manner, is going to be somewhere between the low and medium levels. However, there are going to be some times when you need to increase this quite a bit depending on the kind of dog you are dealing with and the situation that is at hand.

Let's take a moment to unpack the three types of correction that you are going to be able to use, and then we will look at the concept of punishment. We do not condone using the e collar as a form of punishment with the dog, and more forms of punishment, whether they are with the e collar or not, are going to be ineffective and can turn the dog aggressive. We will talk more about that in a bit, but first, we need to focus on the three main types of correction that you can use the e collar for, and these include:

1. Low-level suggestions
2. Medium level suggestions
3. High-level deterrents
4. Punishment

You, as the dog owner, have to decide what level of intensity you are going to work with based on the behavior and how much you want the dog to listen to you.

For example, if the dog is just ignoring you, or they temporarily fix the behavior before going right back to it, then you will want to work with a low-level suggestion. If your dog is about to run away or go into the street of an oncoming car, though, then you may want to the medium level nudges or even the high-level deterrents to get them to stop right in their tracks rather than continuing with the action.

Many trainers like to promote the idea of using just the low-level e collar training with the dog when you need to work with them. This is a terminology that may show up with many companies selling this kind of collar because it is easy to sell the concept to a dog owner who is a bit hesitant about using this training technique at all. But it is not the whole story.

While some dogs are going to be just fine with the lower levels of the collar, some dogs will have to start out at a higher level of corrections and if they are done to improve the quality of life for the dog, and to make sure that the dog does not get hurt or into trouble, then the higher level of corrections is what needs to be done. Most of the time, though, these higher levels of correction are going to not be used on pet dogs, and you really should try out the other two levels a few times first. If those two levels don't seem to be working, then it is time to bring in the higher levels to see if that helps.

In some cases, the higher level is going to work the best for some dogs because if the dog figures out that the collar can deliver more than just a slight tingle of stimulation, then it is more likely that they will be stubborn and resistant. You have to again watch what your dog is doing and how they respond to the collar, and sometimes the level has to change based on your location and the situation that you are trying to put the dog through.

As you can see here, though, we have a fourth component that goes with this, the idea of punishment for your dog. When you are training your dog, punishment is not highly recommended at all, and you should only use it if you find that absolutely nothing else is working or when there are going to be some big implications for the safety and the health of the dog if they choose to not listen to the command.

For example, an owner may choose to use punishment when the dog is charging towards a busy road, ready to chase a dear, or even about to go after a rattlesnake. The punishment is going to be designed to help your dog stop in one stimulation so that they won't do that behavior again. You won't get the luxury of using failed repetition with a rattlesnake like you will with off-leash training or with perimeter training, so the higher amount is used to teach them how to behave fast.

This does not mean that you should go crazy with using this. It is a last-ditch effort to make sure that your dog is going to pay attention to you and that they won't get hurt in the process at all. But other than this, and in the most extreme cases, you do not want to set the level on the collar so high that it is going to hurt the dog. Keeping it at the level that is the most comfortable for your dog, while still getting their attention on you and doing what you want is the most important thing here.

The difference that is going to happen between a high-level correction and a punishment will be the duration of the stimulation. When you use the high-level correction, you are going to do a quick pressure on a higher level, but only if your dog seems to respond to that rather than some of the other levels from your collar.

With a punishment, you may have it at a slightly higher level than normal, and you will hold onto it for two or three seconds to really get the attention of the dog, so they stop and listen to you. Always remember to not use the high-level corrections or the punishments too prematurely. Often the dog is going to listen to you at one of the lower levels, so working with that is the most effective and will make sure that the dog does what you want without getting harmed in the process.

Chapter 9: What If My Dog Faces Some Distractions

Wouldn't it be nice if you could use the collar just a few times, and then your dog would be fully trained, and not even the biggest distraction in the world would be enough to get them to stop behaving? This is a fantasy that you may hope for when you get started with some of the work that we do with this guidebook, but it is not really the reality that you will get to enjoy.

Dogs, as well as most humans, are going to face distractions at some point in their lives. And in the beginning, when the dog is younger and trying to explore and learn about new things, the distractions are going to make it harder to train them. Your goal is to work on minimizing the distractions and to get the dog to follow your commands and your rules even if there is a big distraction coming their way. But in the meantime, before the training is complete, distractions are something that you have to plan for and train against to make the collar training effective.

Reliability in your dog is critical when it comes to training the dog for some pretty obvious reasons. E collar training can be a good way to develop some trust that only seeing can make you believe in. Many dog owners are worried about using this kind of collar to get their dog to behave the way that they want, and they feel that by doing this kind of training or relying on this kind of method, they will end up hurting the dog, turning the dog into an aggressive animal, or not seeing any results in the process.

But working with the e collar is one of the best ways that you can truly get your dog to obey your rules, no matter where you are in the training process, or even what kind of dog you have. Sure, there are some dogs that are more persistent and stubborn than the others, and you may have to take some more time to work with them to get them to listen to you. But over time, with the right use of the e collar, and some other training methods thrown in as well, you will find that the collar can develop trust between you and your dog, and you will be able to get them to listen to your commands, even if there are a bunch of distractions going on around you.

The e collar is a great way for you to be in control. And that is basically what all of the other training methods are teaching you to do as well. You don't want to take this overboard and try to harm your dog, but you do want to train them that you are the one in control and that you expect the dog to listen to you and do what you want.

However, there is one truth that we need to explore a bit in this chapter, one that some people are not that comfortable with when they start with e collar training. But it is something that needs to happen so that you can be prepared any time you go out and for any kind of distraction that may get the attention of your dog. And this truth is that when you work with e collar training, you must go through at some part of the training and put your dog into positions where they will want to ignore some of the commands that you are given.

If you only work on the collar when there are no distractions, it is easy for the dog to listen to you. They have nothing that takes their attention away, and you are the most interesting person at that moment. This isn't going to be the same when you are at the park, going on a walk, or somewhere else that is away from home. And adding in some of these distractions and training your dog on how to avoid and ignore them before they even show up in real life can ensure that the dog is going to listen and follow you, rather than running off or going after the distraction when you give a command.

This brings up the question about what will be the perfect level to use on this collar when the dog is near distractions that may make them not listen to you. As you work with your dog, you will find that there are three e collar levels that will determine how your dog responds to the shock. It is either not enough, just right, or too high. Of course, these are all subjective numbers, and it will depend on the dog you are working with. A large dog will be able to take more than a smaller dog for example.

To make these things even more complicated (as if they weren't difficult to work with already), not enough, just right, and too big change not only with each day, but they will also depend on the level of distractions that your dog is around when you do the training. If you get up in the middle of the night and get a drink of water, and stub your toe on the way, it is going to feel like it hurts really bad. If you startle up in the middle of the night because you hear that someone is getting into the house, and when you go to check it out, you stub your toe. You still feel the pain, but it won't be as bad, and you can still power through to the back door with the pain.

This is the same kind of idea that is going to happen to your dog when they use the e collar and feel distracted by something. Your dog's pain threshold will change from inside to outside, from low distraction to high distraction, and you have to make sure that you fully understand how this changes and what levels your dog may need based on the level of distraction is around them at the time that you use the collar.

As you noticed, when you went from training inside to training outside, the threshold that you have to use probably went up. And then when you head outside to do some off-leash training or some perimeter training, when there was a distraction nearby, you will need to up the levels as well. This may seem like a lot of work in the long run, but it is going to ensure that your dog agrees to listen to you, even if something interesting or fun comes across their path, and they want to run.

Of course, you do have to make sure that you are not putting any mental levels in your mind. If you work with a trainer or find that one number was the highest the dog could handle when you did your initial training, don't let this make you stop if you need to. Some dogs will never really need to go above this higher level. But then there are others who will grow more accustomed to the shock and will decide that going for the distraction or jumping up on people is worth it.

If the dog is behaving in this manner, and you refuse to up the collar, then they are going to start getting out of control and will stop doing what you want. Sure, you don't want to hurt the dog, but this is why you go with the working level that we talked about before. Slowly upping it by one small level at a time will help you to see if this is the problem or not. And as soon as the dog starts responding again and stops trying to take control and go against your wishes, you stop at that level and use that instead.

It is easy, though, to assume that the dog will never go above what we had during the training. But dogs change all the time. As they get used to the collar and the shock or they get bigger and can handle more vibrations, you may have to change up what you are doing. Watch the behavior of your dog and determine if upping the level is necessary or not. If they still respond to you and act the way they are supposed to without going up, then just leave the number where it is. But if they stop listening and see to need it a bit higher, then go ahead and do that as well.

Think of it this way. There are some dogs who are going to be masters of manipulation. This means that if they are able to test you, they will. They like to test you in every way that they can and if they feel that they are able to do what they want without you increasing the level, or if they see that you start to hesitate a bit to press the button to get them to behave, then you are going to end up with some problems. The dog will see this as you letting up some of the control, and you are going to have more problems down the line.

Your job during this process is to make sure that you provide the dog with distractions, in a controlled environment if you can, before they actually try to run away from you due to the distractions. We have talked about some of the ways that you can do this when we looked at the steps used for off-leash training and perimeter training.

You will start out with training the dog on the e collar without going out of the home. This is also a good training process for you because it ensures that you learn how to work with the collar and that you get used to the working level that your dog can handle. Plus, you can get some more practice in with the commands that you have been teaching.

Then you can spend some time outside. Even if you are in the back yard with a fence around you and no added distractions like people or dogs walking around, there will be some distractions that you can work with. The dog will want to jump around and play rather than listen. A bird may fly by. And a million other things will catch their attention. You will have to work with the dog to figure out the right level on the collar to keep their attention and make them listen to your commands the whole time.

Once you have progressed with the backyard, it is time to do some controlled distractions outside of it. You can walk up and down the street in front of your home to get them used to other people. You can even plant some items that you know will get the attention of your dog and then convince them to stay away from those items. These distractions won't hurt the dog if they don't listen right away, but you still want to make it the goal here to just have them listen to you and your commands with the help of the e collar.

When you are ready, it is time for the big challenge. Taking the dog on walks to the park and other places where distractions are going to abound, and making sure that when you want them near you, or you give another command, they are going to listen to you. This one will take some time to build up to, but if you are able to do it, then you will see some great results with the training, and worries about the dog running away or getting in harm's way will be gone.

Determining the right level that is needed to help your dog listen to you even when there are a lot of distractions around can seem tough. You, of course, want to make sure that they are going to listen to you, rather than following that squirrel across a busy street or going after someone else they want to play with. But you also have to balance this with not having the levels too high. And since the levels on the collar will change on a regular basis based on the age of the dog, if they are used to the collar, and where you are with the dog, it is going to take a lot of trial and error along the way.

The best thing that you can do to help with this is to work with distractions from the beginning. You can get the dog a bit used to the collar at home, where you know it is safe. But when you are ready, you will be able to take them outside. And introducing them to a lot of different distractions right from the beginning will make it easier.

This helps you to be prepared when you do go out, and an unexpected distraction comes up. And it lets the dog know that, no matter what catches their eye and their attention, you are still the one in charge, and they need to listen to you. While there may be some other methods out there that you can use to make this happen and to ensure that the dog is going to listen to you along the way, the e collar is going to be the most efficient method for you to use with this one.

Chapter 10: Common Questions Dog Owners May Ask

Now that we have spent some time laying down the foundation of using this guidebook, and how to work with the e collar, it is time to answer some of the questions that a lot of dog owners are going to have when they decide to add this training method to their list of things to work on with the dog. Some of the most common questions that many dog owners like to ask when they are ready to use this collar include:

Will the dog get collar smart?

For the most part, this is not going to be a big issue to worry about. Most trainers will say that if you do a bit of training and laying the groundwork with the commands before you start using the e collar, then the dog is not going to be able to figure out that the e collar is where the stimulation is coming from. However, you will find that if you put the e collar on your dog randomly for three weeks before you even let the unit be turned on, your dog will still get collar smart. Dogs are smart, and they are able to figure out where the stimulation is coming from pretty quickly.

It is pretty much hard to avoid your dog figuring out that the collar is there and that it is the reason they feel the stimulation. It's to be expected that the dog is going to figure out that the collar is the thing that is providing them with the new stimulation, vibration, and tone. Your job though, is to get the dog to respond to the requests that you have with the collar, even though they know where the stimulation is coming from.

How long should I let my dog wear the e collar?

There are going to be two key factors that will determine how long your dog should be wearing the e collar. This is going to include the age of your dog and how consistent you are able to be with your training. Younger dogs are going to be on the collar for longer because the world is new to them, and everything is going to be a big distraction to them that they want to explore. These dogs have yet to check everything out, chase after everything, and take it all in. And this makes them a bit harder to train, and you may have to keep the collar on them for longer than an older dog.

As your dog ages and matures, they will find that there are fewer things around to distract them. They will not be as interested in new things, and there will be fewer things that are new to them, which will mean they need less prompting with the e collar, and they won't need to use it as much. And you won't need to keep it on them as much.

Another key factor to consider is the consistency you use with training the dog in the first place. If you are not consistent with the collar, and you are not consistent with what you expect out of the dog and with some of the other training that you do, then you will find the collar will not be as effective, and you will need to put in more work to see results. You will find that there is a direct correlation between the clients who hesitated when they needed to use the collar and the dogs who ended up having to wear the collar for a longer period of time.

You can't let yourself hesitate if you are going to use this training device. Any time that you hesitate to back up the commands that come with the e collar, you are letting the dog know that they have the option to manipulate you if they want. There are options of training that you can use that won't require you to always push the button to get the shock. But if you need to use the button along with the command because the dog is not listening to you, then you should not hesitate to do this.

For example, a good method that you can use to train with this collar is to say the command and give the dog a chance to listen and obey you. But if the dog decides to not listen to the command and doesn't listen to what you say, then you can use the collar. Sometimes turning on the beeping or the vibration first after they ignore the command will be enough to get them to listen and come do what you want. If they are still not paying attention, then you will do the stimulation to get them to stop ignoring the requests and commands that you are using.

You can work with any type of training program that you would like along with the collar, but remember that consistency is key. If you use the collar some days and not on others, or you hesitate when it is time to push on the button, you are going to end up with a mess. Your dog is not going to listen and you have just taught them that they are able to run the show and do what they want. And this will just make the training a lot harder overall.

How can I transition off using the e collar?

At some point, you may decide that the e collar has done its job, and you want to be able to transition off so that you are no longer using the collar on your dog. The majority of dog owners out there will assume that the collar has done its work too early, and they will then decide to take the collar off their dog too early.

Removing the e collar before the right time can really be detrimental to your goal of having a reliable dog.

It is tempting to take this off too early. You see that your dog is doing well with the collar on, the dog is obeying you and following your commands when you have them on the collar. You assume that this reliability is going to follow as the dog goes off the collar. And then everything goes backward. Your dog sees that the collar is off and doesn't have to respond to the stimulation any longer. And they start to go back to their old habits and not listening or following commands any longer.

When this happens, it is a good sign that the dog was not ready to transition off the e collar. You need to make sure that your dog is really ready, and quitting cold turkey is going to be a bad day. the dog is going to instantly notice that the collar is off and that they don't feel the stimulation, and because of this, they are going to start doing what they want.

A better method to work with is known as the 10+15 method. It is a simple way to help you first determine if your dog is even ready to get off the collar, and then it can walk you through the steps that are needed to ensure the dog can actually go off the collar without reverting back to some of their old ways.

If your dog is not out and about wearing the collar, then it is hard to guarantee the reliability that the dog is going to show when it is time to comply with your commands. It is tempting to wean off the collar when you are ready, but before the dog is actually ready at all. But you need to make sure that you and the dog are 100 percent consistent with the training for six weeks or more before you even think about the transition off the collar.

After the six weeks have gone by, and the dog is listening to you and following your commands 100 percent of the time, it is time to consider working on the transition phase. Your dog will need to wear the collar for this transition period, so don't think that this is a time to take the collar off and throw a party. Doing this is going to cause them to revert back and can mean that you have to start all of your training over again.

For the first ten days of this method, you will only be giving the T/V with your commands. If your dog can make it through the ten days wearing the e collar and you have not had to follow the commands of the T/V with a correction or any stimulation, then this is a very good sign for your training and for taking the dog off the collar. You can then progress to what is going to happen over the next fifteen days. If you find that there were times when you needed to follow up on the T/V command with corrections, then it is not time to transition off, and you should work with this method of training for longer.

Always go at the speed that is the best for your dog. Some dogs are going to be done pretty quickly, and others are going to need more time to adjust and learn how to use the collar and how to behave. If your dog is not able to get through the full ten days without any follow up with a correction, then this is a sign that you need to stick with the e collar for a longer period of time.

Of course, some dogs catch on quickly, and you may be good at reading when your dog is ready to transition off the collar. If you are able to go for the full ten days without any issues, then you can go to the next fifteen days. During this stage, you are going to continue having the dog wear the collar, but your goal is to eliminate the commands from the T/V.

If your dog can do fifteen days straight without any need of the T/V or of the correction stimulation any time that you give a command, then it is time to leave the collar off the dog and in the closet. If you find that any corrections or even just the T/V are needed during this time, then go back to using the collar for at least a few more weeks or more until they are able to pass this test.

This can seem like it is taking a long time, but you need to make sure that it is something that you focus on. Your collar is your best friend for being able to control your dog and get them to listen to the commands that you give. If you take the collar off too soon, and your dog isn't ready to listen to you all of the time, even without the collar, then you are going to run into some troubles. But if the dog passes your 10 + 15 test, then this is a good sign that the dog has passed the training that you have set up with this collar, and it is time to take the collar off the dog.

How can I use this type of collar if my dog has already worn a perimeter fence collar or a bark collar?

Another thing we need to take a look at is if your dog has used some kind of collar in the past, one that is similar to the e collar, though they may work in slightly different ways. Dogs who have experience with a perimeter collar or a bark collar may find that they need to work with a few extra steps during training before they respond to the e collar training. Some dogs who have had training with the other types of collars are going to be a bit apprehensive about the collar, especially if the previous training they received was not that good. You have to keep this in mind whenever you decide to start some of this training with your dog.

Remember that there is nothing that is inherently positive when it comes to the bark collar, so it is likely that your dog is going to really hate them. With the perimeter training though, the dogs are less likely to shy away from the collar by itself because most dogs have learned to associate the freedom of being outside and running around with the collar, so they may even be willing to put it on and learn with it.

We first need to take a moment to unpack a few things that you are able to do to make sure this collar training is a positive experience for a dog who may have had a bad experience in the past. The first thing that you should do here is always put a leash on the dog before you put on this collar. And always bring in lots of treats, praise, and other forms of positive reinforcement so that the dog can start to see that this collar, even though they may be apprehensive about it to start, is going to be a good thing.

When you start out with the training, you may need to take an extra week of training before you go with the foundation period that we talked about before. The reason that you need this extra week or so is because you are trying to not only train your dog how to behave with the collar on, but you are trying to convince the dog that this collar is not a bad thing. Because of the exposure that the dog had to the perimeter training or a bark collar in the past, they are going to expect that the low levels on this collar are going to quickly get more uncomfortable because they have an association based on those other tools that were used on them. This is why this additional step is necessary for this kind of dog.

This step is one where you need to pick out a collar that has 100 levels. If you end up with a collar that only has 10 levels, for example, the jumps between levels are going to be too large, and the dog is going to get nervous and won't help you at all with this kind of dog. You want to go with such a subtle level that your dog is hardly going to show that they even feel the stimulation at all. If you "think" that you see the dog feel the stimulation, then this is the right level to use during this stage.

You don't want the stimulation level to be very high here. The dog should feel it, but there should not be any discomfort or anything. We are not training the dog to listen. We are showing them that the collar is not a bad thing and that it won't hurt them to have it on. This gives the dog some confidence and ensures that you are going to be able to see some results when you use the e collar on your dog.

To help you begin with this additional step, you need to do the most subtle e collar working level that is going to work with your dog. Once you have been able to find this level, you can say your dog's name, and then tap on the continuous stimulation once. Right after this, you will give your dog lots of praise and their favorite treat. This helps the dog to learn that this collar may seem like one that they were put on in the past, but it is easier on them, and it is a positive thing because of what happens after.

You should consider doing this process when you are able to be outside, and even on a walk. You can continue on with the walk, and during it, do this five to ten times or on the whole time. Practice this a few times for the next week before you go through and do some of the foundational training for the e collar like we looked at earlier.

This adds about a week or so to the training period, but it is the best option to use when it is for a dog that has a bad history with some other similar collars. It helps them to see that there is nothing wrong with this collar and that the lower level is not going to jump up and start causing them any harm at all. This will really make your e collar training easier with the dog, especially if their past experience was bad, and they are really hesitant to work with this kind of collar training.

How much distance between me and the dog will be too much for the collar?

Sometimes your dog is going to be ready to run and can start to get away from you. This is pretty normal, especially when they are a puppy and pretty young. You want to make sure that you are getting a collar that is able to handle a little bit of distance in case the dog starts making a run for it. You should be able to read on the description for the item how far it is able to reach.

Some of these collars are going to only be for about half a mile, and this is usually enough. If your dog likes to bounce off quickly, you may want to go with a mile range or higher, but that is meant to work more for a terrain that is hilly or for hunting dogs. You have to determine how far of a range you think that you need for your dog, but it is best if you are able to get one that has at least half a mile on it.

Is the collar going to cause my dog any harm?

The collar in and of itself is not going to harm the dog. It is meant to be a good training tool and can make the dog slightly uncomfortable, but it is not meant to harm the dog. And as long as you make sure to flip it around on occasion, if you plan to leave it on for a long time, then the dog should be just fine with the collar and how it works.

The collar is going to be an inanimate object, and just like any object of this kind, it is going to be subject to the judgment and skill of the one who is using it. If you are not careful with this collar or you decide to work with it as a form of punishment with the dog, then it is possible for you to hurt the dog. When the device is used right, it is not going to hurt your dog at all, and it is going to be a humane and safe tool with a lot of benefits to training your dog.

Think of it this way, though. Even a regular collar and a leash are going to be painful and harmful to the dog if you don't use it the right way and if you get angry and yank at it too much. Yes, the e collar can be harmful and can hurt some dogs if you turn it all the way up or use it in an improper manner.

But if you choose to work with your e collar in a responsible manner, you will find that it is going to be helpful. There is a bit of discomfort that comes with it when it is at the right level, but this is how you are able to make sure that the dog is going to pay attention and do what you want. The only time that the e collar becomes mean and cruel to the animal is when the owner doesn't know how to use it or chooses to use it in an improper manner.

Will this cause my dog to become more aggressive?

There are some dog owners who are not going to use the collar because they worry it is enough to make their dog more aggressive overall. They feel that if the dog is going to feel the stimulation when they try to do something, then the dog is going to take it out on them or on the collar, and then all of the hard work with the training is going to go out the window.

This is not something that you need to worry about if you choose to work with the collar in the proper manner. If you slowly work up to the right working level on the collar, only use it for training purposes rather than all the time, and make sure that the dog learns that the collar is causing the stimulation and their actions are causing the stimulation, rather than their owner, you should not have to worry about the dog becoming aggressive.

Again, this is going to depend on how the user decides to use the device. If you aren't going to pay attention to what you are doing with the product, if you start out at a setting that is too high because you are going to just jump right in without learning about your dog, if you make the dog wear the collar all of the time, or you plan to use this as a form of punishment rather than dealing with it as way to train your dog how you would like them to pay. Use the device properly, and your dog is going to learn how to behave and act the way that you would like. Use it in the wrong manner, and you are going to run into some problems with the behavior of your dog, and the work is going to backfire on you.

Can the collar cause burns?

E collars are going to produce a finely tuned stimulation that feels like it is pulsing. They are not going to be able to produce any heat, so there is no reason that it should be causing any burns on your dog at all. Those who talk about the idea that these collars are causing burns are showing ideas of what happens with pressure necrosis. This only happens when you don't rotate the collar or take it off on a regular basis.

If you are not willing to flip the collar around at regular intervals, and you plan to leave it on for days on end without ever taking it off, then yes, the skin is going to be rubbed raw a bit, and that can be a problem. For those who are responsible owners and who make sure to move the collar around the way that it should, then you will find that the collar is going to work just fine without any kind of burns at all.

Is it really necessary to purchase one of these collars?

This one is going to be a personal preference based on what you would like to do with your dog. There are a lot of different training options that are out there for you to choose, and for the most part, you will be able to properly train your dog without this method at all. With that said, the e collar can make your life so much easier. You will be able to train your dog faster and get them to listen, even without some commands. And if you need to worry about your dog running off or getting harmed, then this is the collar that will help you to get it done.

When you choose to work with the e collar, make sure that this is not the only method that you choose to use with the training. You first need to be able to establish some of the commands that your dog needs to know, or the dog is going to be confused when you add in the collar. But if you use this collar as a training method, rather than as something that is done on its own, you will find that it is much more successful to your goals.

Is a vibration collar a better choice?

The thing is, you can use a modern e collar and find that it does have the vibration feature built-in. This could be as simple as a tap or a pager. Some owners feel that the vibration is going to be better, but for some dogs, and some situations, this isn't going to be true. The vibration, in most cases, is going to have a stronger feel, and to some dogs, it can be jarring and a bit frightening. The stimulation is going to be a sensation that is more subtle, and you can adjust it better than you can with the vibration. This is why having the feature can be nice, but the stimulation is going to be more effective for your raining.

A good way to figure out what your dog is going to feel when they wear the collar is to feel it using your own hand first. You can put it on your neck, wrist, or hand, or anywhere else that you would like to get an idea what the dog is going to be feeling. Just remember here that you are not going to be able to perceive the stimuli in the same way that your dog does.

Some dogs are going to be more sensitive to the stimulation, and you just need to turn down the dial and bit to make it work for them. Then there are some dogs who need it at a higher level before they even start to feel it at all. You have to do a bit of experimenting to figure out the level on the collar that is going to be the best for them so that they feel and notice the stimulation but that it is not going harm them at all.

Do I need to have a lot of knowledge or a high skill level to use the collar?

Anyone is able to use this kind of collar. You may want to read up on the specifics of your collar based on the company you decide to purchase it from. But if you are responsible with the use of the product, and you make sure that you follow the tips in this guidebook, you will find that using the e collar is pretty easy, and you don't need to have any special skills at all.

Is it possible to train my dog how to behave without the collar?

Yes, there are a lot of dogs that are trained without the use of this collar at all. People have been able to train their dogs to follow off the leash, to come when called, and many other commands for hundreds of years without these collars. But the reality is, when this technology was first introduced, it ended up bringing in a bunch of benefits along the way.

The -collar is not meant to replace some of the other training methods that you are working with, and it is not the only method that you are able to use. It is the most effective when you combine it together with the foundations of command training ahead of time. if you are able to do this, then you will find that the dog knows what you are talking about when you give them a command and may respond to the stimulation so much faster.

There is always more than one way to reach your goal. But many dog owners find that using the e collar, along with some of the other training methods out there and a strong foundation of commands and training, is a very effective method to help you to train your dog the way that you would like.

It is going to be up to you how you would like to train your dog and whether you want to work with the e collar on your dog or not. Never let the idea that this is going to hurt your dog or make them more aggressive or call other issues to make you stay away from this great training method. If you feel like another method or training tool is going to be the best for you, then that is fine. But keep in mind that the e collar can be a great option for you to work with and will help you to really get your dog trained faster than before.

As you can see, there are a lot of different things that you are able to do when it comes to working with the e collar and all of the neat things that you can train your dog to do with it. But being prepared and knowing the best steps to take when getting started, how to handle it if your dog has had a bad experience with these collars, or other similar ones, in the past, and how to know when it is time to transition off the collar is going to make a big difference when it comes to how well you are able to train your dog using this method.

Chapter 11: Other Problems the E Collar Can Help You Solve with Your Dog

Training your dog to behave in the manner that you would like is something that takes some time and effort. Many people are surprised by how much work they have to put in to help make sure that their dog is going to behave. But the earlier you start with this, and the more consistency that you are able to add into the mix, the easier this process is going to be, and the more likely it is that your dog is going to always listen to your commands.

There are also a lot of different trading methods that you are able to use when it is time to train your dog to listen to what you want. And one of these methods, one that can really help to keep your dog from disobeying and can speed up the process of training, especially if you are using it along with the other training methods out there, is the e collar. This guidebook has taken a look at some of the neat things that you are able to do with e collar training and some of the different commands that you are able to use.

With that in mind, off-leash training, avoiding distractions, and perimeter training are not going to be the only commands that you will ever want to train your dog to do. There are a lot of problems that can come up with your dog that the e collar is able to help out with, as long as you make sure that you use it in the proper manner. Let's take a look at a few of these and explore just how we are able to use the e collar to help us stop these problem areas and get our dog to behave in the manner that we want.

Stealing food off the kitchen counter

While we may love our dogs, we are not going to be too happy that they try to steal some of the food off the kitchen counter when you turn your eyes away. Your dog sees it as a great treat or some food that should be theirs, especially if they are able to reach it, and it is your responsibility as the dog owner to make sure that they avoid the item and don't try to eat it.

Remember, with this one that when you do decide to tackle this issue, you will not give any commands. If you do try to associate some commands with this one, then the second you leave some food out on the counter and run to the other room, the dog will jump up and get that food item again. You want to make sure that your dog will stop stealing food, whether you are present in the room to watch them behave, or you are in another room.

The steps that you should take in order to make sure your dog knows to never steal food off the counter, and that they can only have the food that you provide to them will include:

1. Put your dog in another room for a few minutes. It can be any other room that you are comfortable with. You just need them to be there while you set things up. It is imperative that you don't let the dog see what you are trying to do.

2. When you are ready, put the collar onto the dog, and double-check that it is turned on.

3. Place a small or medium-sized spoon on the edge of your counter and bait it with something that the dog will like. It is best to use something that has

a strong smell to entice the dog, such as a piece of a hot dog or some peanut butter.

4. Select the right level on the collar based on whatever the working level is for your dog inside of the home, and then add about ten levels to it. So, if your dog usually responds in the home to 13/100, you will want to go with 23/100. If your dog is really sensitive to the stimulation that comes with this collar, it is fine to go a lower amount up to fit their needs.

5. When this is set up, let the dog out of the room you left them in. Take the remote with you when you go into a different room other than the kitchen. Do something like work on your computer or watch a movie there.

6. When you hear the spoon hit the ground, you can hold onto the continuous button for a second, without saying a word to the dog.

7. After the first correction, wait about half a minute and then go get the spoon. Add on a bit more bait and then put it back on the counter.

8. You should increase the level up by ten, or what is best for your dog, each time that you need to set the protocol up again until the dog leaves the food alone.

With this one, you do not need to work with any commands at all. If you do use a command, it is going to set you back, and you will end up with a dog who will still take the food, they will just wait until you are away from home or when you can't catch them in the act. Your dog, by this time, already knows that you do not like them stealing food, so now your goal is to follow through with your control to correct this behavior at a time when they think you can't.

The question that a lot of people are going to have with this one is why they need to start the training at a level that is ten points above the normal working level? The reason for this is that this is one of the situations where your dog will actually be given the opportunity to get something that they want. If you keep the level at a gentle correction, then the dog is not going to be deterred from getting what they want.

The dog wants the food. This is something positive to them, a type of reward to them. And a gentle correction may be uncomfortable a bit, but when it comes to choosing between the discomfort and the great reward of the food, the dog is going to dive right into the food. But when you turn on the collar to a higher level, this is going to become a bigger correction, and the dog is not going to like it.

Now, you may have to go through and up it a few times before you get to the right level to stop the dog. Your goal is to find the level where the dog decides avoiding the discomfort is worth more than going after the treat. When this happens, you will find that the dog is going to stop stealing the food. And if you are able to avoid giving any kind of command when you do this, the training can be quick and efficient, and it won't be long before your dog stops trying to steal food from the counter.

One note to keep with this is that if you are trying to do this training with more than one dog, you may want to get a little camera or use your camera on your computer, to help you figure out which dog needs to be corrected each time. just make sure that it is on mute so that the dog doesn't know that you are on the other side, but it can hurry up the process and make sure that you are getting trained and stop eating food at the same time.

The Dog Eats Poop

If you see that this is happening with your dog, make sure that you talk to your vet to make sure that there are no issues like parasites, incomplete diets, thyroid issues, Cushing's, and diabetes. If the vet has checked out the dog and has eliminated any medical reason that could cause your dog to do this, and you have been able to work on the foundation of training with the e collar, then it is time to work on the steps that are needed to stop this behavior.

After you are done doing the e collar foundation training, it is time to get started. This procedure is not going to need you to use any treats, praise, or even a command because it is an implied behavior. Your goal is for the dog to never do this kind of behavior again.

To start this, you need to have the dog on a long leash. Take the dog out to an area where you already know they are going to find some feces. Start at a level that is ten points above what you usually use with the e collar to start with, and then you can work up from there.

When the dog smells some of the feces and starts to act like they are honing in on the scent, and is about one foot from the feces, hold down on your continuous button for the collar. This should be done for two seconds, but if you find that the dog is not fazed by it and continues on with their intent, then it is time to increase the level. There are some models that you can purchase this collar that allow you to hold down on the continuous button while increasing the stimulation level at the same time.

As you are doing this, make sure that you don't try to say a command. It may come a bit naturally, but remember, you don't want the dog to listen when you use the command, and then go right ahead and do the action when they think that you are no longer watching. If you have a collar that is not able to increase the stimulation level while holding onto the button, you can release the button and then increase the level by ten points (or a point that works for your dog if they are really sensitive to the stimulation), and then re-apply and see what happens.

When your dog does what you want, and walks away from the feces, it is your job to act like nothing has happened because you don't want them to think that you are the one causing the stimulation. As you walk away, consider turning the stimulation down a bit before they get to the next spot. This helps the dog to see that the stimulation gets more intense the closer they approach the feces, and may help them to stay back and away from the issue.

When you see that your dog starts to avoid the feces rather than walking up to it, you can allow them to be off the leash a bit as you continue to watch them. If you let the dog off the leash and you notice that they still take advantage of this as a new opportunity to not listen to you, you can progress by starting at a higher level. After a few days of practicing this, you will find that your dog will stop approaching the feces and this problem will be solved.

Jumping Up on People

The next issue that we are going to take a look at is the idea of stopping your dog from jumping up on others. This is a big issue. Often the dog is not going to mean to be bad or cause trouble, but they are excited to see someone else, and this is the way that they show the excitement. But it can cause issues. You and others who come to your home may not like the dog jumping up. And if you have someone who is older in age that the dog jumps on, it can cause some issues as well with knocking them over.

You will find that the e collar is going to be a great tool to use for this because you can use it to create some distance between those who walk through the door and your dog wanting to jump, and it doesn't require any emotions so you won't have to worry about that getting in the way. The training that happens with jumping on people will be similar to the training that we have done above, but you will do it in a more nuanced manner because while we want the dog to stop jumping, we still want the dog to be social and comfortable with other people when the training is done.

Whether you are doing this inside the home or off the leash outside, the protocol is going to be the same. You want to set the level of the collar at the chosen working level, and then just up it a few levels. Allow a friend or someone else you know to come into your home and instruct them that they should ignore the dog for the first few repetitions.

If during this process, you see that the dog is jumping on them, then you need to hold down the continuous button when they jump and then release it once they stop with the jumping. No one, neither you nor the other person coming into your home should give any command when this is happening because you want the dog to avoid jumping on others whether you are there or not.

You may notice that some dogs are going to be quick jumpers. They are going to jump up on others without much notice, and before you are able to say or do anything, they are all done with the jump. With this kind of dog, you must keep your finger on the button for the collar so that you are ready to push before this big jump happens. In addition, be aware that this kind of dog is more likely to need the level on the collar a bit higher to prevent them from jumping.

Then there are those dogs that like to jump up and are likely to stay there. this process is going to be pretty similar, but you may need to hold down on your button for a bit longer. You can usually go at a lower level as well. In either of the two cases, you may find that the dog decides to ignore you at the lower levels, which means that you will need to do some work to increase the level as it is needed. Remember here, though, that if you do increase the level, and you do it too much, then this will make it so that the dog won't want to approach anyone any longer, and that is definitely not what we are trying to do here.

When you see that your dog is excelling at this kind of training, you can instruct your friend or family member to be a bit more animated with the dog. At this same time, you can put the bowl of treats outside your door for the friend to have access to when they enter, and the dog behaves and doesn't jump on them. If your dog doesn't end up doing the jumping, then your friend can pull out a treat and throw it on the floor for the dog to tell them they did a good job.

You will not want to have other people coming to your home and training your dog, which is why we are doing this step now. If you do this training process in the right manner, other people can then come into your home, as loud and excited as they would like, and your dog will sit and wait until they want to pet the dog, rather than having the dog jumping on them.

Pulling on the Leash

The next thing that we need to look at when it comes to training your dog is when they try to pull on the leash. This is a big issue that a lot of dogs are going to face when they first get started, and it is one that you are able to break within a few weeks if you decide to go out on walks enough and work with some of the training techniques in this book.

If you have already gone through and done some of the foundation work for this collar, and even tried some off collar training, but you still find that the dog gets excited or wants to pull against you and the leash, there are a few more methods that you are able to use to make this work.

One technique that is used often for these persistent pullers is known as the stop and pop method. With this method, you are going to take the dog out on a walk with a leash that is about six to eight feet long. You want to go with a leash that is at least this long because it gives them more room while you do the training.

At the moment, right before the dog starts pulling on this leash, you will need to stop quickly and tap on the continuous button at the exact same time. A good level with this one is to set it at 10 levels or so higher than what you know the working level to be. If you find that this is not enough and the dog insists on pulling against the leash, then you can increase the level some more until you have a dog who is walking, but also leaving some slack on the leash.

This is just one of the techniques that you are able to use with your dog. Another option for pulling on the leash is the pressure/release technique. With this one, you are going to add on a low to medium level continuous pressure every time that the dog starts to pull. Then, when they stop pulling on the leash and allow for a little bit of slack, you can stop pulling. You can adjust the levels on the device based on what works for your dog.

Remember that this means that you will probably need to use the shock a bit more on the dog until they figure out what is causing it and what will make it stop for them. Some people don't like to work with this method because you end up pushing the button more. But for some dogs, this is the method that is going to work the best for getting the dog to listen to you and do what you would like.

How to Work with More Than One Dog at a Time

Another thing that you may have to encounter when it is time to work with training with this collar is if you have more than one dog at a time. when you are trying to train more than one dog with this kind of collar, it is often best if you are able to train each dog on their own, at least until each dog is doing well. When they are doing this, you can start to work on the dogs at the same time. You will need to be patient with this and remember that when you are training two or more dogs, it is going to take some time to help you get adjusted and to make sure both will behave.

While you are doing this, keep in mind that the collar is going to only deliver stimulation to one collar at a time. this means that you cannot press two or more stimulation buttons at the time because the radio frequency that comes with it is going to block both signals.

This can be a pain if both dogs are causing issues for you. If you find that both dogs are running away from you and you would like to call them both back at the same time, you have to get the attention of just one. Picking out the dog who is leading the chase and getting them to turn around can often help make this work better.

Predatory Chasing

This process is going to be simple, but as a new trainer, it is easy to make it too complicated with unnecessary and complex protocols. You need to start out by determining which animals you are fine with your dog chasing around, and which animals they should not chase. It is probably best if you are able to prevent them from chasing any animal at all so not to bring in confusion, but you can really pick out which animals are fine and which ones are not.

When your dog happens to see an animal that they are not supposed to be chasing, you can say come, wait for a second, and see if they are going to come back to you. If they don't, then you can hold onto the continuous button on the collar. It is best to start this one with the normal working level, and then you can increase the level as needed if you find that the dog is not responding to you or not.

If the dog is not responding to the controller that you have, you may have to dial it up pretty quickly. More times than not, you will hear your dog vocalize a bit and then stop. Once this happens, you will be able to call the dog back, and you should not use the collar for this part. Once the dog comes back, turn down the level on the collar and continue on with the walk. Or, you can have the choice to put the dog back on the leash if it is needed at this point.

This is a process that is best done on an e collar that has the versatility to hold down the continuous button and increase the level all at the same time. it is best if you are able to continually hold down the button, and then increase the level quickly until your dog stops. If the collar is not able to increase the level without releasing the button, then you need to be able to give the command, hold down the button, release the button, increase the level and then reapply.

How far should my dog be able to range away from me?

This is going to depend on what you are comfortable with, how well your dog is at listening, and the area you are in. For the times when you are in an area that is not safe and has a lot of traffic, and so on, then you will want to keep the dog closer to you. But when playing in the park or somewhere safe, and you know that your dog is good at listening, then it is fine for you to let the dog get a bit further away.

You will find that at the beginning of your training, it is best if the dog is not allowed to range too far from you. As the dog is better at training, you can choose if you would like to let the dog go further. For the most part, the dog is able to keep within fifty to one hundred feet to make the training effective. The best idea though in all cases, is to make sure that the dog never gets out of your sight at all during the training, and otherwise, so that you can watch for anything that may cause them danger.

Training your dog with the e collar is going to be something that takes you a little bit of time to do. And it may seem like you have to almost restart with all of the different behaviors. But over time, you will get used to working with the collar, and your dog will learn the drill. And before you know it, the dog is going to start behaving, and you won't even need to use the collar any longer.

Conclusion

Thank you for making it through to the end of *E Collar Training*, let's hope it was informative and able to provide you with all of the tools you need to achieve your goals whatever they may be.

The next step is to get started with this method of training and ensure that it is the right one that you and your dog are going to stick with. There are a lot of methods of training your dog, and the e collar is not meant to replace any of them. It is meant to make sure that you are able to properly train your dog, along with some of the other methods that you may decide to use.

If the e collar is part of your training plan, then it is time to go and purchase one of these collars for your dog. You can then try it out by seeing how to get it to fit on the dog, and seeing which stimulation level is going to work the best for them. This guidebook is full of the information that you need to make this happen, and to ensure that you are able to get the collar to work properly for you and your dog. Once that is all set up, you will be able to go through and work on some of the training examples that we listed to get your dog to do what you want, whether you are there or not.

This guidebook spent some time talking about e collar training and all of the neat things that you can do with it. When you are ready to make training your dog easier, and to enhance some of the other training methods that you may be using, make sure to check out this guidebook and see exactly how e collar training can work for you!

Finally, if you found this book useful in any way, a review on Amazon is always appreciated!

Puppy Training

A Step By Step Guide to Positive Puppy Training That Leads to Raising the Perfect, Happy Dog, Without Any of the Harmful Training Methods!

Jenna Jimenez

Introduction

Congratulations on purchasing *Puppy Training,* and thank you for doing so.

The following chapters will discuss all of the things that you need to know in order to get started with training your new puppy. Bringing home a new addition for the first time can be a really exciting endeavor. The whole family may have spent time picking out the puppy that they wanted to bring home, and now they are excited to bond with her and to make some lasting memories.

But before this happens, you need to make sure that you train the puppy in the proper manner. This is the best way to ensure that the little one is going to be able to avoid having accidents, does not get aggressive, and is able to follow the commands that you give to them. Once this is all in place, your puppy will be a valued member of the family, who also behaves and acts in the manner that you would like.

This guidebook is going to walk you through the steps that you need to follow in order to get your puppy trained and ready to behave. To start, we are going to prepare for the puppy by getting the supplies to make her feel at home. Then we will move on to some of the things to expect when you bring the puppy home the first few days with the puppy, the golden rules of dog training, and some of the basic stages that you need to keep in mind when you start to train a new command to your puppy.

Once we have some of those basics down, it is time for us to move into some of the actual training methods that you are able to use. We will look at crate training your puppy, how to house train your puppy, and some of the reasons that positive reinforcement, rather than negative reinforcement, will be so important when it comes to all of the training that you decide to do with your puppy.

To end this guidebook, we are going to move into some of the fun commands that you can teach her. Even if we miss a few that you want to work with or some of the tricks that can be used with your new puppy, you can still use tips and methods that we discuss to work with those commands as well. We will finish off with some tips on how to deal with any separation anxiety that your puppy may have when you or someone else in the family leaves, and how to deal with some of the tough dog problems that can sometimes develop in a new puppy in your home.

Bringing home a new puppy is meant to be a great experience for the whole family. But you can make it even better when you stop and train her on the behaviors that you see as acceptable and the ones that you would rather they learn how to avoid. When you are ready to learn some of the basics that are needed to train your puppy, make sure to check out this guidebook to help you get started.

There are plenty of books on this subject on the market, thanks again for choosing this one! Every effort was made to ensure it is full of as much useful information as possible. Please enjoy!

Chapter 1: Preparing Your Puppy

Getting a new puppy to add to your family can be an exciting thing. Whether you are getting your first dog, and you want to make sure that they can acclimate with others in your home, or you have had a few in the past, and you want to make sure you get it right this time and that there are no issues between the different dogs in your family. No matter the case, this is a time that needs a bit of preparation. There are a few things that you will need to get organized before you bring home the new puppy to ensure that you are prepared and that everything goes as smoothly as possible.

Budgeting for the Puppy

If you are truly ready to bring a puppy into your home and raise them, make sure that you don't overlook the financial part of the process. One of the biggest mistakes that a new dog owner is going to do is to adopt a new dog without properly budgeting for the recurring costs that a dog is going to generate. It is best if you are able to come up with a god budget right from the start, before you even bring the puppy home, to ensure that you are fully aware of how much it will cost and whether you are able to fit this into your life right now.

The Preparation List for Your Puppy

The next thing that we need to take a look at is how to prepare for the puppy. As part of the budgeting process that you are trying to work with, you are going to need a few supplies to make things easier. You should consider purchasing some, if not all, of these items before your puppy comes to your home, to make sure that you are set and that the puppy is going to feel right at home with you. Some of the items that are going to be important includes:

1. The dog crate

2. High-quality dog food

3. Food and water bowls

4. Treats that can help you with training

5. Any toys that you would like to use with them.

6. Items to chew on so that they won't have to chew on furniture or shoes.

7. Leash, collars, and harness

8. A baby gate if you want to keep the puppy in one area of the house.

9. A brush for the dog

10. Toothpaste and toothbrush for the puppy

11. Ear cleaning solution

12. Bath supplies like nail clippers and shampoo for the dog

13. Poop bags for when you go on walks.

14. Treat pouch and carrier if you would like to have this.

15. First-aid supplies

16. Tick, flea, and heartworm protection.

Let's take a look at some of the things that you need to have and some of the different reasons that you would want to use these items.

First on the list is the crate. The crate can be important to use because the puppy is going to be a den animal, and they thrive when they have their own space to feel safe and secure. It is important for their well-being to have a safe place where they can go in order to relax. It is also great for the behavior of your puppy and their mind. It allows them to get away from the things that are going to distract them and make them feel nervous and can be a good restart place for them. And the crate helps to make house training your puppy so much easier.

When picking out the crate that you want for your puppy, the size of the dog is going to matter. A small crate is going to make the puppy feel squished, and they won't enjoy it as much. But getting a crate that is too big for the puppy can be hard on them as well. Pick out a size that is perfect for your puppy to feel safe and relaxed in, but not large enough to run around in.

The next thing that we need to look at is the dog food. You need to pay special attention to the foods that you provide to your puppy because it will help with the dog's physical and mental development. There are a few different kinds that you are able to choose from here, and they include:

1. Raw feeding: This is going to be a diet that relies on raw foods for your dog and allows the digestive system to eat what is all good for them, rather than the processed foods. This is usually more expensive to work with, but if you are able to do it, you will see some great results.

2. Kibble: This is the method that most people are going to work with because it is easier and less expensive. There are some great kibbles out there, but you do need to double-check the kind that you are using, stay away from any that have added color in it, make sure of all the ingredients that are inside, and stick with kibble that is grain-free. There are plenty of natural and nutritious options to choose from. Do your research and see what you can afford for your pup's health.

Once you have picked out the kibble or food that you want to use, it is time to pick out the right water and food bowls to use for your pet. When it comes to the water and food bowls, it is fine to use any kind that you would like, except for any that are made out of plastic. The reason for this is that your puppy is likely to chew on the plastic, and this leaves you with a lot of destroyed bowls and the possibility that the puppy will have swallowed some of the plastic. Note also that some dog breeds may need a bowl that sits higher off of the ground.

Training treats are going to be your best friend as you work to train your puppy on the right way for them to behave. You will need a lot of these in the beginning. It is best to go with softer treats because these are easier to break apart, so you don't go through as many. There are a lot of good treats out there that help with training, just read up on the ingredients to make sure they are safe and healthy for your puppy.

And of course, you want to make sure that your puppy has some of their own toys. If you don't provide them with these toys then you are going to deal with the puppy finding their own, and this could be your favorite pair of shoes, your sofa legs, or something else that is valuable to you. Make sure that you pick out toys that are specifically designed for a puppy. There are some kids toys that may look the same, but the manufacturers of these are not going to assume that their products will be used by a dog, and this could be dangerous depending on the pieces on that toy.

Always monitor your puppy when they are playing with any of their toys. Dogs, especially when they are young puppies, have a common tendency to chew through and destroy their toys. Don't forget that they are teething! They like to rip the toys apart, which can be a normal part of their play, but if you are not watching for things it is possible that the puppy will ingest a small part, some of the rope, the stuffing, the fabric or another part that they should not. Monitoring the puppy ensures that you are going to be able to catch them if this starts to happen.

Chewing toys are next on the list. These can be separate from the other toys and are meant to help the puppy as they feel the urge to chew on something. It is much better to give them some kind of toy to chew on, rather than letting them use their own imaginations and chewing up the house. There are many objects that are acceptable for your puppy to chew on, and they will help them to fulfill their need for chewing while keeping the gums and teeth of your puppy as healthy as possible. You can pick out the kind of chew toy that you would like your puppy to have, but a few of the options that are available for you include:

1. Antlers: these are amazing chewing toys for a dog. They are hard, they last for a long time, they are all natural, and they will have the minerals and vitamins that your puppy needs.

2. Bully sticks: These may not last as long as the antlers, but they do last a lot longer than some of the other chewing options out there, they are natural, and they are going to be full of vitamins that the teeth of your dogs need.

3. Himalayan dog chews: These are going to be a healthy kind of chewing object that is made out of Yak's milk. They are going to last a bit longer than the bully stick and can be a nice alternative.

4. Bones: It is possible to work with bones, but you need to be careful with them because they are going to be easier for the puppy to break apart and can cause issues with your dog. If you are going to use these, be careful because you don't want to go with ones that are too soft, like cooked bones, and you want ones that are not going to fall apart.

There are other options when it comes to the chewing toys that you are able to give to your dog, but you do need to exercise some caution with these. You want to pick out ones that are natural, ones that are going to be strong enough to last for a long time and ones that maybe have the added vitamins and minerals that are needed to keep the teeth and gums of your puppy as healthy as possible.

Now we need to take a look at the collar, harness, and leash of your puppy. The collar will come first. There are a variety of collars that you are able to purchase, and each of the styles that you see will serve us with different options, Out of the four most common options that you can go with, the ones that are the most recommended are going to be the first two:

1. The simple collar: This is the common collar that is plane, maybe in a single color, that is flat and will connect with a buckle or a clip to your puppy.

2. The martingale collar: This one is a bit different because it is designed so that the puppy is not able to slip from their collar. It is going to gently tighten around the neck when the dog is pulling on the leash, which can be a good bonus when training.

3. The choke collar: This one is generally not recommended. If it is not used in a proper manner, it can be harmful to your dog, especially when they are still a puppy.

4. Prong collars: This one is almost going to pinch the puppy, which is not the best way to teach them how to walk on a leash. They are not going to be effective, and in some cases, it is going to result in them become more aggressive.

Once the collar is picked out, it is time to take a look at the harness. The harness can be a great tool when you are trying to teach your puppy how to walk on the leash in the proper manner. The harness is going to help with the pulling, helping you to slow them down without adding on so much pressure to their neck, and allows you to control their whole body as well. There are several types of harnesses that you can choose based on the one you like, and what is going to fit your size of dog.

The leash is next on the list. You need to have a leash to help the dog learn how to walk around the block any time that you want. There are two options, but most dogs are going to work with the standard leash for the most part. These are easier to work with, come in different sizes based on your type of dog, and so much more. You can also work with a retractable leash, but many people find that this kind can go against what they are trying to do when it comes to training the puppy.

A brush is next on the list. No matter how long the coat of your puppy is, the brush is going to make sure that they are well cared for, that the old hair is removed, and that the new hair is able to grow in well. The type of brush that you decide to use on your dog is going to vary based on the texture and the length of the coat of the dog.

The other things that you may want to consider adding into your home to help you prepare more for bringing the puppy home include:

1. Toothpaste and toothbrush for a dog: Dental hygiene is going to be an important part of the process of raising your new puppy. You should start

brushing the teeth of your puppy from the moment that you bring them home, even though they are going to lose those first teeth. It is also best to work with a dog-specific toothpaste and a two-sided toothbrush. Do not feed the dog human toothpaste because the fluoride inside can be bad for dogs.

2. Ear cleaning solution: You also need to add in some weekly ear cleaning when you bring home the dog. There are many choices for this at a pet store in your area. Make sure to get some cotton balls and other items to help make this process easier.

3. Dog shampoo: Dog fur is going to be different than human hair, so you should not use soap or any human shampoo to bathe them. Dog shampoo is always the best because it has been created with the dog in mind.

4. Nail trimmers: You also need to spend some time trimming the nails of your dog on a regular basis. If you choose to do this on your own, make sure to get some dog nail trimmers to make it easier.

5. Poop bags: Unless you want to keep using a lot of plastic grocery bags and you want to make sure that you always have enough on hand, make sure to purchase some poop bags.

6. Treat carrier: This is going to be an optional part of the process, but it is nice so that you are able to easily grab out the treats any time an opportunity to train your puppy comes up.

7. First aid supplies: Think about some of the first aid needs that your dog may have, and then make sure to keep these on hand. There are even a few

companies that make first aid kits that are meant for dogs, and you can pick one up and keep it around in case you need them.

8. Tick, flea, and heartworm preventatives: It is very necessary for you to have these preventative treatments. They do cost more, but they are a very simple measure that can be taken in order to make sure that your puppy stays healthy and doesn't get a bad disease. You can get these at many pet stores or talk to your vet to see which ones are the best for you.

As you can see here, there are a lot of different items that you will need to get in order to work with a new puppy. And it is best if you can get it all gathered up and ready to use before you bring the puppy home. Having this all set up and ready can help to reduce some of the stress that you may be feeling when bringing a new puppy home, and ensures that you will be set and ready to put your love and attention on the new addition to your family.

Chapter 2: Bringing the Puppy Home

Now that you have had some time to gather up the items that are needed for your puppy, it is time to prepare to bring the puppy home. Having a good idea of what is going to happen during the first few days with her, and how you can make the transition a bit easier, will make a world of difference. Let's take a look at some of the different things that you need to prepare for when you finally bring the puppy home.

The First Three Days

Remember that when you bring a new puppy home, the life that they once knew and were used to is going to change up completely. Every dog is going to react to this kind of change, but it is important to know some of the different issues that may occur when you first bring the puppy home.

The first issue to be aware of, and that you should just resign yourself too now is sleepless nights. Puppies are similar to babies in that they are going to keep you up for the first few nights. They are going to bark and perhaps cry for the first few nights, and sometimes longer, until you have been able to crate train them all of the way.

In addition to the sleepless nights, be prepared for the puppy to have accidents. Even if your dog is a bit older when you bring them home, it is possible that they will have an accident, simply because they are in a new place and they are not sure where they should go. Be prepared for this and don't feel upset when it does happen. The puppy needs to learn the rules that are allowed in your home so that you can all live together peacefully.

Rules for Feeding Your Puppy

In the beginning especially, you should make sure that the feedings happen in the crate for your puppy. There are a few reasons for this. First, most puppies are going to be motivated by food, and feeding them in the crate is one of the best ways to get them used to that area. Plus, the crate is a great place for the puppy to be able to sit down and digest their food. To avoid any issues with digestion, puppies should get a rest after they eat. Keeping them in the crate helps to make this happen.

You have to be careful about free feeding the puppy. There are some people who like to use this method to ensure their puppy will get as much food as they need. This advice is bad for the health of your puppy, and can really affect how well you will be able to train your puppy. There are a few reasons why free feeding your puppy may not be the best idea for you or for them, and some of the reasons will include:

1. It can make it easier for your puppy to become overweight. Many puppies are like humans, and if you put out a big bowl of food in front of them, they are going to eat it, even if they are not hungry.

2. When you have food available to them all of the time, it makes the crate and food less appealing. This can take away some of the power of the training treats.

3. It is important for you to keep track of how much your puppy is eating at each meal to make sure they meet their nutritional needs.

4. It is going to lead to you having more accidents. When you are not in control over the feeding times, then it is hard to monitor when your puppy will need to go outside. When you are in control of this, you can learn their patterns and get them outside faster.

5. It makes it harder for you to monitor the healthy habits of your puppy for the long term.

Just like monitoring the food that your children eat, you need to make sure that you are monitoring the food that your puppy eats. Some puppies are going to be light eaters or will be pickier than you would like. But just know that they will warm up to the food if you give it time. Some of the steps that you can use are to only leave the food in the crate for about 15 minutes or so, and then take the bowl completely out of the crate at this time, no matter how much the puppy has eaten. And don't offer any food to the puppy until it is mealtime again.

There may be times when you feel a bit bad about taking the food away and not offering it back to your puppy until it is the predetermined meal time again. But you will find that the puppy will not starve themselves to death if they have food in front of them. If they were hungry, they would most definitely eat it when it is in front of them.

Acclimating the Puppy

Finally, being able to bring the new puppy into your home can be a really exciting thing for the whole family to enjoy. However, there is going to be a little bit of stress that comes with brining the puppy into the home as well. The best thing to consider here is that the puppy is going through a lot of change. While the dog is going to adapt to these changes much faster than most people do, it is still going to take them a few days to get used to being away from their mother and siblings. Luckily, there are some actions that you can take in order to help your puppy adapt and get ready to take on some of the new environments that they are in.

First, we need to make sure that we are checking out the essentials. Make sure that, before you bring the puppy home, you figure out what they did before you got them. Depending on the time of day you bring the puppy home, you may want to figure out the last time that they were able to eat, and when they were able to go potty.

When you get home, and before you even bring the puppy inside, take them to their designated potty area outside. Let them have some time to explore. This is a brand new area for them, and they may want to figure out what is there and take note of their surroundings. Give them about five minutes or so to see if they will go potty.

Once they have had some time to go potty outside, bring the puppy into the house. You probably do not want to introduce them to each room of the home at this point. Your home can seem really big to a new puppy, and it may really scare them in the beginning. It is best to bring them to the puppy corner and let them have some time to become more familiar with the crate.

Even though the puppy is brand new to your home, it is important to start training them on the right kinds of behaviors from the beginning. It may only last for a few minutes, but put the puppy into their new crate with either a chew toy, or some food if it is eating time, as soon as possible. If you find that the puppy doesn't seem to be that interested in what you are offering, offer some new toys or treats until they like something enough that they will be willing to interact with it for a few minutes.

The point of doing this process right away is to help the puppy know more about the crate and get more comfortable inside of it. If you do this introduction to the crate properly, the puppy is going to immediately associate the crate and your home in general with positivity, and this is going to set you up for a great start as time goes on.

Recognizing Some of the Stress Signals

Each dog is going to be different and unique. None of them are going to react in the same manner to the same things all of the time, and that is just fine. The trick here is to learn the personality that comes with your puppy, so that you are able to react to them and give them the love and attention that they need.

With that said, it is also a good thing if you are able to understand some of the body language that your puppy is sending to you, especially if they are stressed or uncomfortable around you. Your goal, especially in the beginning, is to learn how to recognize when the puppy is feeling stressed out and worried, so that you can step in and try to make them more comfortable.

So, this brings up the question of how can you tell when the puppy is feeling stressed out? You will find that the puppy is not going to be like a person, and they won't be able to just come up and tell you that they are feeling anxious or stressed out. As the owner, you need to be able to recognize some of the symptoms that show how the puppy is feeling a bit stressed out and worried. Some of the signs that will show you that your puppy is stressed out will include:

1. Stress yawning: This is going to be a bit different than what you are going to see with a tired yawn. It is going to be done in a more intense manner, and it will be done on a repeating basis.

2. Licking of lips: This happens when there is no food around at all.

3. Pinning ears back: The puppy may decide to have their ears lay down and point a bit behind them.

4. Avoidance: This is when the puppy is going to turn their head away, or they will try to move away.

5. Excessive panting: If you notice that the puppy is panting quite a bit without being hot or tired, this is a sign that they feel a bit stressed out.

6. Growling: This is a very easy indicator to look for. If your dog is growling, then this means that there is something that is causing them to feel uncomfortable.

7. Tail in a lower position: The tail is out low or in between the legs. You may see that only the very end of the tail is actually wagging.

8. You see that the dog starts to bite at their own paws. This is going to happen almost out of nowhere, and the reason that it is happening is that the puppy feels a bit uncomfortable in the situation they are in.

If you bring home the puppy and you see that they are exhibiting a few of these behaviors, then this means they are feeling stressed out and uncomfortable about the situation they are in. it may be time to look around and see what is making your puppy feel this way. Does your puppy see another dog? Do they hear a noise that is loud or unusual? Are there a lot of strangers that are approaching them?

It is pretty natural for the puppy to be nervous when you first bring them home. They are in a new place, surrounded by a lot of new faces that they are not going to recognize at all. Giving the puppy some space to explore and look around, and being there when they need you will help them to grow more acclimated to the area. However, if you have had your puppy for some time and you notice these signs start to come up, then it is time to see what is causing it and figure out what you can do to make it better.

Always remember to not scold your puppy when they are dealing with these kinds of emotions. You may not like the emotions and they may be a bit annoying at times, but this doesn't mean that the puppy is doing anything wrong. They are feeling nervous or worried about something, and they aren't sure how to handle the situation. Learning what triggers your puppy and what you can do to desensitize them a bit so it doesn't bother them or removing them from the situation, can help. You may also find that with crate training, your puppy can regulate on their own because they know the crate is a safe spot all their own, a place they can go any time that they need a break or that they need a bit of comfort.

Bringing home a brand new puppy can be an exciting experience for the whole family. Maybe you have been planning out bringing home your own puppy for a long time, and now you finally get to do it! Make sure that you are prepared for the first few nights to be a bit hard to get adjusted to, try and learn a bit about the personality of your puppy, and learn how to tell when she is feeling stressed out or uncomfortable. The first few days are a great chance for you and your puppy to bond together, and giving each time to learn about one another can make this so much easier.

Things to Consider About Grooming

Another thing that you need to consider when you bring a puppy home, is how you are going to groom them. Some owners decide to do the grooming on their own in order to save some money, but others like to give that job to a professional groomer in order to get the results that you want. Both of these methods are going to be just fine, as long as you make sure that the puppy gets regular grooming to keep them healthy.

One of the biggest and most costly misconceptions that come with raising a puppy is going to come with grooming and the significant investment that it is going to require on the part of the owner. There are two main problem areas that a lot of dog owners are going to fall into when it comes to grooming and these will include that they are going to ignore doing any grooming on their puppy completely, or they instill fear into the puppy when grooming is done because they have very little knowledge and grooming protocol.

The first group is going to be those who decide to ignore the grooming of their new puppy completely. When a new dog owner brings home a puppy and finishes with some of the training that we will talk about in this guidebook, they may come to the conclusion that they have met all of the basic needs of the puppy and as long as they feed the puppy, it will all be good.

Make sure that as a dog owner, you don't become this kind of person. It is so important to the happiness and the long term health of your puppy to make sure that they are well groomed at all times.

Then there are those who are going to instill some fear into the puppy about the grooming and will make them feel like grooming is the worst thing possible. This is often because they don't know what they are doing or they don't understand what is going to happen with the grooming. They want to make sure that the puppy is going to be happy and behaved during it, but you need to make sure that you follow all of the steps that come with this.

The first thing to consider here is how to make sure that you get the puppy as comfortable as possible before all veterinary and grooming activities. Some of the things that you can do to make this happen include:

1. From the time that you bring the puppy home, make sure that you touch them on all the body parts so that they get used to it. This can make them feel more comfortable, and prevents aggression and fear when they go to get groomed. Touch their head, open their mouth, touch the nose, ears, feet, legs, and more.

2. Doing this is going to help the puppy be more used to all of that touching so that they are more trusting and more friendly to others who groom them and try to take care of them.

Now, there are going to be a lot of different grooming needs that your puppy is likely to have. whether you decide to bring the puppy to a groomer that you trust, or you decide to do it all on your own, there are a number of grooming activities that should be done on a regular basis. You want to make sure that the puppy gets their ears cleaned, that the fur is brushed, their teeth are brushed, they get a bath, and nail trimming is done as well.

You can do some of these on occasion at home, but many dog owners like to still set up some regular grooming sessions to make sure that the puppy is getting all of the right care and attention that they need. This also helps to make sure that anything the owner may miss in terms of their health or of the grooming will be caught. If you choose to have a groomer help you with some of these items, make sure that you pick out someone who is reputable, and who will take good care of your puppy in the process. Scheduling the grooming sessions every few months, or even a few times a year, will help the puppy get more used to this process, and will cut out some of the anxiety and other problems that can come with it.

While grooming may be something that a lot of owners are going to overlook and forget to work with, it is so important for the health and the happiness of your puppy. If you feel comfortable with doing this on your own, you can certainly do it to save some money while still taking care of the puppy. If you don't have the time, or you are worried about doing any of this on your own, then finding a high quality professional groomer can make it easier, while still ensuring that your puppy will get the care and attention they need, and the healthy grooming that will help them as well.

Chapter 3: The Golden Rules of Dog Training

Now that we have adjusted a bit to the idea of what we need to get and how to bring home the puppy and get them more comfortable in their new surroundings, it is time to take a look at some of the rules that you can follow when it is time to train your puppy. You may not start training the puppy, the second that you bring them through the door of your home, but the sooner you start training, the better it is for the whole family. That is why we are going to take a look at five rules that every family with a new puppy should follow. These will make your life easier, can help the puppy adapt to their new home, and will ensure that you can get them trained to follow your house rules in no time! Let's take a look at these five rules and how you can make them work for you.

Use Positive Reinforcement for Everything

The idea that comes with positive reinforcement is that you need to send out a lot of rewards to your puppy when they perform the behaviors that you do like and that you want them to repeat. You can pick out the rewards that you would like to do, including treats, toys, affection, or anything else that your puppy tends to respond to and see in a positive manner. This concept is simple to use, but many families spend too much time on negative reinforcement, and then wonder why their puppy is not responding.

This one is going to require a lot of attention from you in order to get the results that you want. Any time that you notice the puppy is sitting calmly, focusing on you when you do tricks, or behaving in any other manner that you want them to, take the time to reward them with your chosen method. The bigger deal you are able to make out of it, the more likely it is that your puppy will continue on with this kind of behavior in the future.

The trick here is to make sure that you are not rewarding the negative behavior. If you ignore the puppy when they are sitting quietly and doing what you want, but then jump up and start making a lot of loud noise and being mad when they chew on the couch, guess which behavior the puppy is going to want to repeat? This is not the kind of reinforcement that you want to encourage

Associate the Name of the Puppy with Lots of Positivity

It is always a good idea to say the name of your puppy in a positive way. If you do need to scold the puppy, do not use their name. When the puppy responds to you saying their name, even if it is as simple as looking in your direction or coming over to you, tell them "YES" and then provide some kind of reward. This is a good thing to get into the habit of because it helps your puppy to learn early on that hearing their name is a positive experience and that they are going to get a reward of some kind when they hear it.

You may think that this is a silly thing to work with, but when you establish with the puppy that calling their name is a positive thing, then you have taken the first major step needed in order to establish some recall habits that are strong. Then, later on, when the dog is off the leash, and you see that they are about to run off to another dog or go away from you, you will be able to get them to come back and stay with you by saying something as simple as "Rover, come!"

The opposite is going to be true if you try to say the name of your puppy in a scolding tone. If you have done this for a long time, then any time you try to use it in the future, even when doing some training, the puppy is going to wonder if they are going to get a reward or going to get in trouble. They may decide that it is not worth the chance of getting the reward, and they will run off and not listen to you.

Don't Get in the Habit of Repeating the Commands

Any time that you are giving a command to your dog to do something that you want, make sure that you are just saying the command one time. When this is enforced in the proper manner, it teaches the puppy that they need to perform that command right away after only hearing it once. You don't want to start out the training by having to tell your puppy to "sit' a bunch of times before they actually listen.

Now, this is where the positive reinforcement needs to come into play again as well. But if there are times when the puppy doesn't go through and perform the command right after you are done giving it, especially in the beginning when they are learning the process, there are a few steps that you can take to make this easier including:

1. Try to reinforce the hand gesture that you want to associate back with that particular command.
2. Say the dog's name, a kissy sound, or some kind of sound that will get the focus of the puppy back to you and the hand gesture that you are using here.
3. Learn how to be patient. You do not want to repeat the command, but the puppy Will perform the wanted command if you have patients and get them to focus on you again.
4. When the dog does go through and perform the command or action that you want, be sure to tell them "Yes" right away and provide the reward that you want.
5. Always follow through with what you are asking your dog to do, and remember lots of consistency, and you will be set.

Remember here that if your puppy is not listening or they are too distracted when you give the command, and you have gone through the steps that we have listed above, do whatever it takes to get the puppy to listen to you. You could try to do something that the puppy will find more fun and motivating, lure them over to you with the help of a treat, put them on a leash, or use another option that works the best. No matter what you do here, remember that you do not give this up. This helps the puppy to learn that they need to listen to your commands each time, with no exceptions along the way.

Try the Power of Redirection

Whenever you find that your puppy is doing something that they should not, such as chewing on an object that they shouldn't, you need to tell them "NO" and then find a way to redirect the puppy over to an activity that they are allowed to use. So, if the puppy is chewing on an item that you don't want them to, say "no" and then move them over to one of their chew toys or something else that you will let them have.

Any time that you see the puppy showing a behavior that is annoying or that you won't allow, redirecting them over to something else is one of the best ways to make sure they learn what is and what isn't the appropriate behavior in your home.

Too many owners get into the habit of just telling their puppy no, and then they don't add in the redirection to the mix. This is just going to cause the puppy to feel really confused, and they are not going to really stop performing the behavior that they were told to avoid in the first place. This redirection is going to give your puppy the motivation that they need in order to stop doing the behavior.

Training Needs to Always Be Fun

Yes, training your puppy to behave in the manner that you would like is going to be tough. But you also need to make sure that there is an element of fun found inside the training as well. If you are not having a good time, and your puppy is not having a good time, the problems are going to start showing up, and it becomes a lot harder for you to get the results that you would like.

It is best if you are able to make the training of your puppy as fun and happy as possible. This helps the puppy to get excited about the experience, and this is the motivation that they need to listen to you and do what you want. Also, when planning out the training sessions, remember that your puppy is going to have a short attention span, so do not get frustrated when you have done this for some time, and the puppy stops listening. Keep the training sessions short and sweet, and fun and your puppy will catch on to what you would like them to in no time at all.

Learning how to train your puppy to do what you want may sound like a lot of hard work. You may be worried that you are going to do it the wrong way, or that your puppy will not respond to what you are telling them or doing along the way. But with these five golden rules in place, and some of the other tips that we are going to discuss in this guidebook, you will find that training your puppy won't just be a necessity, it will be something fun that you and the puppy enjoy doing together, and will help your puppy become a valued and behaving member of your family.

Chapter 4: The Stages of Training a New Command to Your Puppy

At this point, you may have a great plane in place to start training your puppy. You know some of the rules that you need to follow to ensure that your puppy is going to start listening to you and that you both have a fun time when you get going. But at some point, you will want to learn how to teach a new command to your puppy.

Over the time that you have your puppy in your home, it is likely that you are going to want to teach your puppy a lot of different commands, and you want to make sure that it is as easy as possible to work with. That is why this chapter is going to take a look at the top five stages that you need to follow in order to ensure that you can properly train your puppy any new command that you would like.

Stage 1

The first stage that you need to use when it is time to train a new command to your puppy is to show a hand gesture to lure the puppy, and then reward them with a treat and a clicker word. During the beginning of your training, remember that your dog is still learning, and they are working to understand and follow some of the commands that you want to teach them. The basics of the process that you want to work with during this stage include:

1. Give the hand gesture that is meant to go with the command that you would like to teach.
2. Say the command verbally.
3. Lure the dog in some manner to the position that you would like to command them to go.
4. When the puppy listens, it is time to reward the puppy using the clicker word and the treat. Make sure that you do this each time that the puppy performs the command in the proper manner.

Stage 2

Now we are on to the second stage. This one is where you are going to show the puppy the hand gesture, and then when they respond, you will reward the puppy with the treat and the chosen clicker word. Over time, the puppy is going to start making the connection between the hand gesture and the verbal command and his body position. When this happens, it is time to cut out some of the luring that you need to do.

This part is going to take a bit of patience from you. You need to try it a few times and be ready for the puppy to make some mistakes along the way. Your goal here is to give the hand gesture along with the verbal command and then give the puppy a few seconds to see if they will respond to it without the luring. As with all parts of the training, as you move through all of these steps, you are going to be surprised at what the puppy is able to accomplish with a few chances and some patience from you in the process.

Stage 3

Now it is time to move on to the third stage of the training process. In this one, we are going to show the gesture, and then we will reward with the treat and the clicker word every other time. You do not want to go for ten years having to give the puppy a treat each time they listen to a command that you give. You want them to be able to listen to the commands that you give without having to give them any treats in the long run. This is where we are going to start doing this process.

Once the puppy is able to do the command right away, each time that you command them (both verbally and with the hand gesture), you will want to reward them with the clicker word, but slowly you are going to take the necessary steps to wean the puppy from the treats. This means that you will stick with the clicker word, but you will cut out the treats a bit. Start just giving the treats out every other command.

One mistake that a beginner needs to be careful about is going too fast with weaning off the treats. If you are still uncertain about whether the puppy is ready for this step or not, it is best to go with the treats as a reward for each time you do the command, at least for now. It is so much better for you to reward with treats for a longer period of time rather than nixing the treats too quickly.

Stage 4

The fourth stage of the puppy training process is to show the hand gesture and reward with the clicker word while tricking with treats. This is an important step that you need to get to at some point because it ensures that the dog is going to learn that they need to listen to what you are saying, rather than them just listening to get the treat. No matter if you are holding the treat up so that the puppy can see it or not, you want to make sure that the puppy learns how to be motivated by pleasing you.

So, how are we going to make sure that this will happen? Basically, to make it happen, you are going to present the treat as usual, and then, once the puppy does the command, you will reward them with the clicker word and praise. You can also do this the other way as well. This means that you would have the puppy do the command just by holding up the chosen hand gesture. Once they execute the command, the treat is going to come out of nowhere (your pocket, but it will seem like a surprise).

This is an important thing to try out because it will keep the puppy guessing about whether they will get a treat for doing the command or not. And by default, if this is done at the right time, it is going to help the puppy transition from being motivational with getting a treat all of the time to being motivated without any kind of treat in their face. This is the ultimate goal that you want to reach in order to really see the puppy listen to you, even without a treat present to entice them.

Stage 5

Now we are on to the final stage. With this one, we are going to show a hand gesture, and then we will reward the puppy for listening to the command with a clicker word and a treat on occasion. Once you have been able to get the puppy to consistently listen to the commands that you are giving, you have actually been able to master the hardest part that comes with the training. From this point on, you will want to always work with the clicker word each time that the puppy completes the command that you want, but the treats should be used sparingly by this point.

The point here is that you do not want to have to provide the puppy with a reward in the form of a treat each time that they listen to you. This is going to get more tedious overall, and makes it so that the puppy is only listening to you because there is a treat involved. You need to slowly wean away from the treats so that the puppy is going to respond to what you want them to do, regardless of whether they get a treat or not.

You can add in a special treat on occasion, but you should get to the point where you will be able to get the puppy to listen to any command that you say. If you follow the five stages from above, you will be able to make this happen with your training sessions with the puppy.

A Note About the Clicker Word

We spent a bit of time in the last section talking about a clicker word. You have probably seen people who are at the pet store training classes that use a clicker to help them train their puppy. If you are not sure what this is all about, a clicker is going to be a little device that will make a clicking noise any time that you push down on the button. When you are training the dog, the goal here is to make the clicking noise any time that the puppy gives the right behavior, and then pair it up with a treat.

Now, this method may work, but then you have to make sure that you have the clicker on you all of the time. Other people like to use a clicking sound with their voice instead. Your voice is going to be with you all of the time, and this makes the process a bit easier. But you can choose whether you want to keep this clicker around with you, or you want to use a clicking sound with your voice for this training method.

Another thing to consider here is whether you are able to use a good boy or good girl for the clicker word that you use. You can choose to use this, but for the most part, you will want to stick with words that are one syllable long. And you want to make sure that it is some word that you won't say all of the time. If you are able to do this, it is a lot easier to add the clicker or the clicker word, along with the treat, to the end of a command to make sure that your puppy is going to do what you would like them to.

Training your puppy is a process that you and the puppy need to work on together. It is not going to happen overnight. But if you are willing to work through it with your puppy, and you use the five stages and a good clicker word, or even a clicker, like we talked about above, you will be able to really see some results in no time with how well your puppy is going to behave and listen to the commands that you give.

Chapter 5: How to Crate Train Your Puppy

One of the biggest mistakes that you are able to make when you are doing some of the training your puppy is to not crate train them. It is going to seem like a lot of work, but it is going to make your life, and the life of your puppy, so much butter. It does take some patience for you in the beginning, but once it is all done, you will love how easy it is to work with your puppy and provide them with the love and attention that they need.

Some people feel that crate training is going to be a bad thing for their puppy. They feel that it may be inhumane or a punishment or even cruel. But this is not true. In fact, crate training is going to provide the puppy with a safe spot, someplace they can go when it seems like things are getting too much for them. By crate training your puppy, you are basically giving them a safe place that their ancestors have evolved over the years to depend on. Anybody who is telling you that crate training is wrong simply doesn't understand the benefits that this method is going to provide, not just to you but also to your new puppy.

However, one thing to remember here is that your puppy, even though it is good for them, is probably not going to be that fond of their crate at first. They may whine, howl, yell, bark, and more, especially when it is near to the time for bed. And this can end up being frustrating. You have to hold strong here because if you give in, the puppy is going to continue this behavior and won't do the crate training for you.

The number one rule that you have to follow when you are doing crate training is to not allow the puppy out when they are making noise. You do not want to let them out for any kind of noise or sound, whether it is howling barking, or whining. You may think that letting them out is one of the best ways to get the puppy to be quiet and settle down. But this just makes it harder for you to do the training because it basically rewards the puppy for this bad behavior.

Think of it this way. If the puppy doesn't like the crate and whines and barks a bit to get let out, then you let them out, what do you think is going to be the behavior that they will continue doing? Letting them out because of the noise just enforces the behavior that they were just doing, and if they don't like the crate and they want to get out, they will continue on with the behavior. But, if you make them quiet down before you let them out of the crate, they are going to learn the opposite. They will see that being quiet and settling down is the best way to get out of the crate, and then you can let them out when you are ready.

Your dog is going to respond to the crate in their own unique manner, based on their own disposition and if they have had any experience with a crate in the past. The person who was previously in charge of your puppy may have already had a chance to start with crate training, especially if the dog is a bit older. But if you have a brand new puppy that you just brought home, then this may be the first time they have ever seen the crate.

Now, there are times when the puppy may have been exposed to the crate in the past, but it was not in a positive manner. If this has happened, then you are going to have to approach the crate training in a slow and cautious manner. You may have to take things a bit more slowly compared to other dogs to make sure that they see this as a safe spot to be in.

The best thing that you can do when you work on some crate training is make sure that you associate as much positivity with the crate as possible. This crate is meant to be a safe spot for the puppy. It is their place to go to rest or when they need a break or to get away from things that scare them. You do not want to start using this as a form of punishment.

Yes, sometimes it is tempting to use this as a way to get the dog to behave or as a form of punishment when you feel mad that they chewed up your furniture. However, doing this is going to ruin all of the efforts you have made to make the crate a safe spot. The negativity is going to cause the puppy to only see the crate as a form of punishment, and they will not want to go into it any longer. So, the thing to remember here is to only use the crate in a positive manner.

The next thing that we need to explore here is how you plan to get the puppy into the crate and start to use it. Even if your puppy is not that averse to the crate in the first place, you will find that they probably won't run into the crate the first time that they see it. Because of this, you will need to go through and convince the puppy that the crate is just fine to be in, and that it can act as their own little den.

The good news is that you are able to use food as a positive tool here. Since almost all dogs are going to be food motivated, dog food is going to be a positive tool that you can use to your advantage in order to get the puppy to the crate. Feedings, in the beginning, need to take place inside the crate. Many puppies will see the food in the crate and will run straight there to get the food. And before long, when the puppy is hungry, they are going to run over to the crate and wait to get their food over there. If you are consistent with feeding the puppy in the crate, they are going to quickly catch on to this kind of behavior.

Of course, it is possible for you to use some other items to associate some positivity to the crate. This can include some of the chewing objects or some toys that are popular with your puppy. Treats can also be another positive thing that you will hand to your puppy if they go into the crate. You do not want to leave the toy or the chewing item alone in the crate with the puppy unattended because this runs the risk of the puppy ripping the toy open and ingesting something that they should not.

The next question that you may have when it comes to crate training is how much time you should leave the puppy inside the crate. While there isn't really a concrete number of hours that you should use the crate, but you should have the entire day of the puppy revolve around the crate, rather than having the day of the puppy revolve around being out of the crate and being free to roam around the house.

This is going to make training the puppy so much harder to do overall. When the puppy can move around wherever they want, this makes it more likely that they are going to have accidents, will destruct many of your personal items (or any that they are able to get ahold of), and you will have a big headache from trying to figure out where your puppy is and where they may decide to go next.

When you decide to allow your puppy to have free reign of the home, they are going to take full advantage of this. This is why creating a structure and setting boundaries for your puppy right from the beginning, so they learn right from wrong, is so important. It is easy to let things slide when the dog is still a cute little puppy, but the sooner that your dog learns the rules and adheres to the principles in your home, the sooner they will be able to gain the freedom to roam around your home later on, without you having to worry about the kind of trouble they will have.

After you have been able to use the crate training for some time, and you are sure that your puppy understands what behavior they are allowed to do, you can then begin the transition of your dog, leaving the crate and gaining more freedom. This process will take some time, and the length of time that it takes is going to depend on the dog and their disposition as well. Some dogs may do just fine if you start to give them some more freedom, and others are going to start misbehaving after you give them some of the freedom. If your dog stops listening and starts causing problems when you make this transition, then it is time to get them back in the crate and work with the structure for a longer period of time.

With this in mind though, wherever the dog happens to be with their training for the crate, it is important that you never use the crate as a way to punish the puppy when they do misbehave. It may be tempting to do this at times, but it is going to disrupt the process of training, and it can really make all of the hard work that you have been doing go to waste.

The whole purpose of working with the crate is to provide your puppy with an environment that is calming and secure for them, a place where they are going to feel safe. But first you have to make sure that they feel comfortable inside the crate, and that they don't feel like it is a punishment. Most puppies want to be able to move around and have the freedom, and so they won't be happy to go into the crate. Taking the time to turn the crate into a positive thing, and ensuring that they learn how to use this crate for their own personal space, is going to make life easier.

You may have to take this in stages. It is not a good idea to bring the puppy home, have them just a few days, and then leave them for 8 or more hours in the crate without any exposure. This is going to seem like a punishment since the puppy is not used to the whole process. Crate training is something that takes some time because you have to slowly teach the puppy to get comfortable.

You may start out with five to ten minutes in the crate. You leave the puppy in there for that time, and at the end, you get the puppy to quiet down before letting them out. As soon as you let the puppy out, allow them to have a treat and lots of praise and playtime. This is a good thing to include in your process because it shows the puppy that they are supposed to go into the crate and behave. Just make sure that you don't let the puppy out when they are whining or barking or misbehaving, or this is the behavior that you will become used to seeing when the puppy is in the crate.

Then you will slowly expand the time that they are in there. From the ten minute jump up to half an hour, then to an hour, then to a few hours and so on until the puppy is able to stay in the crate for the whole amount of time that you want them to be there. Each time that you come back and let them out after they quiet down, give them a treat of some kind and lots of praise. And if the puppy has to stay in the crate for a longer period of time (say that you built them up to a full day of eight hours), make sure that you let them out to the bathroom and take them out to play and run off some steam since they have been so good.

The most important thing to remember here is to not give in to the whining or the howling or the barking. Your puppy is not going to like the crate in the beginning, and they want to be able to get out of the crate and explore. This can cause a mess. If you give in to the whining and the other issues, then this teaches the puppy that this is the right way to behave, and they won't do what you want in the future. If the whining and howling and barking are too much for you to handle at this time, just walk outside and wait until the time is up.

There are a lot of advantages to using the crate training. It can be hard. You don't want to seem like you are mean to the puppy by having them stay in the crate all of the time, especially when they are young, and you are just forming your bond. Remember, this is not causing them any harm, and they just need to have a bit of time to adapt to this new routine.

Once the puppy sees that this is a positive place to be, where they can find comfort, and they get food and fun toys, they will start to go there all on their own. They will start to find that this is the place where they want to be, even when they are given more freedom. And this is also a good step to take to help with many of the training things we will talk about, especially with potty training, because you will find that once the puppy establishes the crate as their den, they will be less likely to want to mess it up or make it dirty. Leaving them there during the day with this idea can help to train the puppy to listen and go outside rather than in the house.

Sample Schedule of Doing Crate Training

We spent a bit of time talking about some of the benefits of working with crate training with a new puppy, and some of the steps that you can take in order to make sure that the puppy starts to love their crate and sees it as a positive thing rather than as a punishment or something that is negative. As we also mentioned, it is best if you are able to make sure that the puppy, at least in the beginning of their training, like the crate and has their day revolve around this crate. But how are we supposed to make this happen? Some of the steps that you can take, or a sample of the schedule that you can use, in order to help you get the day of the puppy to revolve around the crate is going to be as follows:

1. Puppy wakes up in the morning already in the crate and then is sent outside to go potty.

2. After this time, the puppy goes back into their crate to enjoy some breakfast. You should let them stay in there for half an hour to an hour to allow the food to digest before they run around.

3. After this time, the puppy will be taken outside to go potty again.

4. Since you have taken the puppy out to go potty, you shouldn't have an issue with having an accident inside. This means that you are able to allow the puppy a bit of freedom here. You can have some supervised playing where you play with them, or you let them wander around and play with some toys, but you are right there.

a. Since the puppy is out of the crate and hasn't been house trained yet, you can take them out ever twenty minutes or so while they are out of the crate to ensure they don't have an accident.

5. After an hour or so of playing, the puppy can be put back in the crate. Leave a chewing object with them for a few hours.

6. Before you feed the puppy lunch, take them back outside to go potty for a bit.

7. Feed the puppy some lunch and let them rest in there to help with the digestion for the next twenty to thirty minutes.

8. When lunch is done and has some time to digest their food, take them outside to go potty again.

9. Allow the puppy to have some more time to play, but keep them under your supervision for this time.

10. When it is time, add your puppy back into the crate. They are likely to want to take a nap during this time, but you can also leave a chew toy in there for them in case this is what they would rather do.

11. After the nap time, the puppy needs to go outside to go potty again. If there is time, you can let them have a bit of time to play.

12. It is time for dinner now. This again should last for about twenty to thirty minutes depending on how long your puppy needs to digest their food and rest.

13. After the food has time to digest their dinner, take them back outside to go potty.

14. Now it is time to let the puppy play for a bit. Keep them under your supervision to make sure that they don't get hurt in the process or cause problems. This is a great time to practice some tricks if you want to do this, or just for the family to play with and explore with your puppy.

15. Before you get ready for bed, take the puppy back outside.

16. Tuck the puppy back into their crate for bedtime. You may also need to take the puppy outside a few times at night to go potty, but this depends on how old the puppy is at the time of the crate training.

Chapter 6: On to House Training Your Puppy

Now that we have had some time to look at the benefits of crate training your puppy and some of the steps that you need to take to make this happen, it is time to take a look at the basics of house training your puppy. For many new dog owners, house training is going to be seen as one of the hardest parts of raising a puppy. However, if you are consistent and do it in the right manner, you will find that a lot of the time commitment and the frustration will be gone. And this is where we are going to start ourselves off with this chapter.

Before we dive in, though, remember that your puppy is going to be an individual, and they will respond to the training at their own pace. There are tips and tricks that you can use that will make the practice a bit easier, but for the most part, each dog is going to respond at their own pace. Don't be persuaded by the marketing pitches of training programs that say how your puppy has to be trained in six days or less. Sure, there are some puppies that can learn quickly, but most will take a bit more time.

What we mean here is that you should not come to this step with a timeline or expectations that are unrealistic. Understanding that your puppy is going to be unique in the manner that they can respond to the training is going to put you at ease and will give you the right mindset to actually get through the house training without a lot of frustration along the way.

The first question that a lot of people have when it comes to house training their puppy is when they should get started. The best option here is to be prepared to begin some kind of house training the moment that you bring the puppy home. Follow these guidelines in order to train your puppy in the fastest way possible and minimize the number of accidents your puppy has in your home.

The first step that you take is to show your puppy the area that is designated for the potty, and this is where you will need to place the puppy each time that you take them outside. The puppy will obviously not go potty in the exact spot each time, but taking them over to this spot when you bring them outside will make a difference. Eventually, the puppy will catch on that this is the spot they need to use to go potty if you do it enough times.

The amount of time that your puppy is going to be able to wait before they have to go outside and go potty will vary based on their age. If you have just brought home an eight week old puppy, then being consistent and taking them out to go potty on a regular basis is going to be the best bet. This is going to be the way that you teach them where and when to go potty faster than before. In fact, one of the best ways that you do this is to take them out to go potty every twenty minutes when they are not in their crate.

Now, there may be times when you bring home a puppy that has been with their past caregiver for some time. It is easy to assume that you don't need to take the puppy outside as often when they are older, especially when they were doing well with their previous home. Of course, you need to remember that when the dog comes home with you, they are in a brand new environment, and they are pretty much starting things over. You may not want to go every twenty minutes when the puppy is older and house trained, but do not go over an hour when they are outside of the crate until they adjust to the new place.

This may seem like a lot of times to take the puppy out, but the more that you do it, the quicker they are going to learn about this process, and the quicker they are going to get house trained. The shorter the amount of time between the breaks to go potty, the faster the house training will go. This results in a puppy that learns the rules of the home faster and will help you to have fewer accidents.

Another tip that you may want to work with while training your puppy is to always bring some treats outside during the potty break. This way, when the puppy does go potty outside, especially when they do it in the designated area like you show them, they can get praise and a reward all at the same time, reinforcing what you are trying to teach them.

The next question that a lot of people are going to have when they work on house training their puppy is what they should be doing when they take the puppy outside. Remember that the routine that you set up is going to be the most effective method to use to reduce the time it takes to train the puppy. When you establish a consistent routine that is associated back with an activity, it is going to start ingraining itself as a habit in the cognitive processes of the brain.

The routine does not have to be super complicated in order to work for your needs. A good routine that can help you to speed up the house training process between you and your puppy could include something like the following:

1. When it is time, you can take your puppy outside to the designated area for going potty.
2. Tell them the command of "go potty."
3. Once the puppy does go potty, give them a treat to let them know that they did something good when they were able to go potty outside. Make sure to give the puppy treats or some physical affection and a lot of praise when they do decide to go potty outside.

It can be as simple as that. In addition to following the steps above for house training, crate training can go hand in hand with house training, and they can work to make the process work better for both of them. One of the keys, in fact, of this is that each time you take the puppy out from the crate, take them right outside to go to the bathroom. If they end up having some accidents in the time they walk from the crate to the door, then you may need to carry the puppy outside so that you don't end up with this kind of issue.

Now, you need to make sure that you are not letting the puppy stay in the crate too long when you are potty training. Most puppies are going to have an instinct to keep their area or their den clean. This isn't going to happen around the house because they can just go and walk away from it. But when you keep them in the crate, they do not want to dirty up the area around them. You can use this to your advantage to work on potty training because the puppy is going to be less likely to have any accidents in the crate.

The problem is that you could be tempted to leave the puppy inside the crate for too long. The puppy has a small bladder, and they are not going to be able to hold it in for 8 hours or more at a time. If you do end up needing to leave the puppy in for longer, then you need to make sure that you or someone else stops by and lets them out once or twice during the day. This helps the puppy to get some relief and will reinforce what you are trying to do with your house training.

You may also run into the issue of the puppy taking a long time to go potty when you take them outside. The first thing to remember here is that you need to be patient. Sometimes the puppy gets distracted and wants to look around and explore the world around them. This causes them to not go potty the second that you take them out, even if they have been stuck in the crate for a long time period before this.

You may find that you need to wait for about 15 minutes or so. The more time that you give the puppy to go potty in the beginning, the faster they will go potty once outside, and the faster you can get the house training done. This may seem like it is going to take forever, and you may be impatient, but just think of how much faster it will make the whole house training process. In the beginning, these 15 minutes may need to be expanded out to 30 minutes or more for the best results.

If you take the puppy outside and wait 15 to 20 minutes and they don't go potty, bring them back inside. Put them back into the crate for a bit, maybe ten to fifteen minutes, and then take them back outside. Repeat this until the puppy does go potty outside, and then give them a big treat and a lot of praise for doing a good job.

This can be hard, and it is going to take a lot of your time in order to see the results. But this is the best way for you to get the house training done. It is also crucial that you actually make your way outside with the puppy and watch them go puppy. This allows you to tell if you are actually getting the puppy to go when they are outside. Over time, the puppy will get the process down, and you will be able to give them the freedom to go back outside and inside any time that you would like.

Of course, if you have a young puppy, there are times when an accident is going to happen inside during play time or the few times that you keep the puppy out of the crate. As the owner, you need to watch how you react to the accident that the puppy is having. This is going to make a difference in how successfully the house training process is going to be. If you catch your puppy going potty in the house (and if you have a young puppy it is going to happen), then you can do the following steps;

1. Run over to the puppy as quickly as possible.
2. Say "No" in a firm voice to the puppy and then pick up the puppy.
3. Bring the puppy outside right away and bring them out to the area you designated as the potty. Give the command "go potty" to them out there.

It is important that you move quickly during this time. running is the best. Whenever a puppy is about to go in the house, sprint over to them and see if you are able to catch them before they even start. Even if the puppy is already going potty, get to them as quickly as possible and still pick them up. The puppy will stop going as soon as you pick them up, so don't hesitate here and then take them out to their potty spot as quickly as possible.

Now, there have been a lot of false options that have been given on what to do when your puppy goes potty inside. These things are going to reinforce a negative behavior at best and can make the puppy aggressive in the worst. Some of the things that you need to make sure that you never do when you see your puppy going potty inside include:

1. Scold the puppy for an accident that you did not personally see them do.

2. Just watch your puppy when they have this accident without doing anything to put a stop to it.

3. Yell or be really aggressive in the manner that you use to scold the puppy.

4. Put your puppy into the crate as a form of punishment for having the accident. Remember, the crate is not supposed to be a form of punishment for your puppy.

5. Rub the nose of the puppy in this accident.

Out of these myths, the first one about scolding your puppy for an accident that you didn't actually see being done is the most common mistakes that dog owners will make. They may come into the room and see a pile of poop or a puddle of urine in the house, feel upset about this, and then will go on and scold the puppy for doing this. But you have to remember that when you do this, the puppy is really going to have no idea why they are in trouble. they won't even remember that they went to the bathroom in the house, and this scolding is not going to benefit either of you. Yes, it is unfortunate that they did this, but at this point, you need to just clean it up and move on, working to prevent it the next time that it happens.

Being able to debunk some of the myths about house training your puppy is so important to this guidebook. Often we think what we are doing while training the puppy is for the best, and it ends up undermining all of the good things that we try to do. Even if you have made some of these mistakes in the past, though, you can follow the tips in this chapter and in the whole guidebook to make sure that you avoid this problem and get the best results with house training your new puppy.

Chapter 7: Using Positive Reinforcement to Get What You Want

While this chapter is going to be brief, it is important to take a moment to explore why using positive reinforcement in all that you do with training your puppy is going to be so important. There are too many owners who are going to focus on negative reinforcement, often without realizing what they are doing, and then they wonder why the puppy is not responding to what they say, or why the puppy is not doing what the owner would like.

As a new dog owner, you will find that the method for training dogs that is the most efficient and the most effective is going to be the use of positive reinforcement. Positive reinforcement is the idea of seeing the behavior that you want in a puppy, and then rewarding it with praise, treats, and other rewards. This shows the puppy that they are doing an action that you approve of. And since the puppy is getting this reinforcement from you and seeing that they are doing things properly, they are going to be happy to keep on with that behavior.

Let's take a look at a quick question here. What do you think would make you more determined and excited to complete a task?

1. Would you be more motivated to complete a task that you were praised for doing correctly?

2. If every time a task was assigned to you, you were automatically given a negative stimulus until you completed the task. Once the task is done, you see that the negative stimulus is gone, but there isn't any praise for the work that you did?

It is probably pretty safe to guess that most people are going to find that the first example, the one where they get the praise for completing the task at hand, is the one that they would find enjoyable and the one where they would strive to actually complete things.

The first example is going to show us what positive reinforcement is all about. But the second one is going to show us what negative reinforcement is all about. Just like you would respond to the first one, your dog is going to respond to the positive reinforcement as well.

The reason that they are going to respond to this is that the puppy knows that they are going to be given some kind of reward, whether it is a treat or some praise or something else when they complete the task. This is going to give them the motivation that they need to do the task and complete it over and over again. Plus, the positive reinforcement is going to make sure that your puppy is having a lot of fun with the training and will keep the puppy in good spirits while you do the training.

Examples of Positive Reinforcement

The best way for you to get the puppy to do what you want during training and other times is to focus on positive reinforcement. This is a bit different than what you may have seen with some of the training that your parents and others did while you were growing up. But it is more effective and can go a long way in helping you to get the puppy trained faster and more effectively. As you may have noticed if you used any negative reinforcement on your puppy before this kind of thing is going to reinforce some negative behavior that you probably don't want the puppy to have.

When you use positive reinforcement, you are going to focus on training the puppy in a positive way. Basically, when the puppy does something that you want, you are going to praise them, give them a reward, and make sure that they get a lot of attention. The point of this is that when you provide the positive reinforcement, the puppy wants more of it, and they are going to connect the positivity with that action, and they are going to do more of it.

Of course, this is not instant. The puppy is learning, and they are going to be a bit impulsive in the beginning. This means that you may not be able to get them to obey and listen the first few times that you use this behavior with them. But, the more you do it, the more consistent you are with it, and the more elaborate the praise, the faster the puppy will learn.

There are some different options that you can use when it comes to positive reinforcement, and the choice is going to be based on what seems to work the best for you. For example, some people find that working with lots of praise and petting will work. Some rely on treats. And others may provide some other kind of reward to your puppy.

A note on the treats, though. While these are going to be powerful motivators for your puppy, you do need to be a bit careful with them, especially if you are already working with training commands to your puppy. You don't want to fill the puppy up with these treats and make them miss out on their meals because they are too full. This is why using some other positive reinforcement options, for the most part, can help to keep your puppy healthy. If you do throw in a treat on occasion for really good behavior, that is fine. Maybe break up the pieces a bit so that the puppy still gets something, but doesn't fill themselves up too much on the treats between meals.

Positive reinforcement is going to be a much better option to go with when you are trying to make sure that your puppy does the actions that you want. It does take some time, and you need to have a bit of patience when you are using it. But it will result in faster and more effective training methods than using any other type of reinforcement when you work with your puppy.

Examples of Negative Reinforcement

Many dog owners who run into trouble when it comes to training their puppy, find that it happens when they use negative reinforcement. This happens when we use negative experiences in order to try and train their puppies. This is going to either reinforce the puppy to do the behavior that you don't want, or it can make them more aggressive in order fight back against the behavior.

Sometimes the negative reinforcement is going to be on purpose. If you are hitting your puppy, rubbing their nose in any accidents that they have, or even spraying them with a spray bottle of water to get them to behave, then you are using negative reinforcement, and it is likely that you know this. And if you don't realize that this is negative reinforcement, then it is time to stop and correct those behaviors right away.

Other times the behavior may not be something that you realize you are doing. For example, if you scold the puppy or get mad when they chew on the furniture and when they have an accident in the home, you are using negative reinforcement. Your first instinct may be to yell and get mad. But all this is doing is showing the puppy that they are able to get attention this way, even if it is negative attention. This gets worse if you ignore the puppy when they are doing the good behaviors that you want and only giving them attention when they are doing the bad things.

In some cases, you may find that it is going to make your puppy more aggressive when you use negative reinforcement. It is going to teach your puppy that they need to act out against you to get you to stop the yelling or the hitting or the other options.

Whether the negative reinforcement is done intentionally or not, it is still a good idea for you to learn how to make it stop and focus instead on working with positive reinforcement. This encourages the puppy to behave in the manner that you would like rather than encouraging them to act in a way that you don't really approve of for them.

Which One Is the Best?

As you should be able to see with some of the different examples that we have been talking about with reinforcement, it is easy to see why positive reinforcement is going to be the best. For some people, this may seem a bit strange, and they may not know how to change up some of the habits that they had before in order to deal with this new option. But in reality, if you want to hurry up the training process, see better results, keep the training session fun, and make sure that you don't encourage behaviors that are bad or an aggressive behavior from the dog, then it is best to stick with positive reinforcement.

Remember, when you add in some positive reinforcement to the training sessions that you do, this is not only going to make it more fun for your puppy, but it will make things more fun for you during the training sessions as well. Plus, think of how great it is going to feel when your puppy is fully trained and acting just like you want them too!

Chapter 8: The Top Commands to Teach Your Puppy

This chapter is where we get to some of the fun stuff about training! We are going to look at some of the steps that you can take in order to teach your puppy some basic commands. There are a lot of different commands that you are able to teach your puppy, but we are going to focus on some of the basic ones that will make your life with your puppy a little bit easier. Some of the basic commands that we need to take a look at include:

Sit

Teaching your puppy how to sit can be a stepping stone to making sure that the puppy is a well-trained dog. When the puppy can sit on command, it helps them to learn some self-control. This method of teaching your puppy to sit is going to teach them how to sit down physically, but can be a good way for the puppy to learn how to calm down mentally and engage their focus on you. Before you try moving on to any other trick or command, make sure that your puppy has mastered sitting. Some steps that you can use to help with the teaching of the sit command includes:

1. Have the puppy face you. Tell the puppy to "sit" while you hold out a treat in the hand position of your choice.

2. After saying sit once, you are not going to repeat the word again.

3. Put the treat to the nose of your puppy.

4. Move the hand so that it goes slowly forward, from the direction you are in, towards the dog as if you are going to move the treat over the head of the puppy.

    a. The reason that we do this is that it is an automatic way to get the puppy to lower their butt as they try to get to the treat.

5. Once the puppy has their butt on the floor, you can reward them using the treat and the clicker word.

6. During this process, it is important for you to go at the pace of your puppy, and you need to keep the treat on their nose. Also, never force the puppy to sit down by pushing their butt onto the floor. This isn't going to teach the puppy anything since you are forcing it, and it can cause some harm to the hips of the puppy if you are too forceful.

7. In the next fifteen to twenty minutes, repeat this exercise as many times as the puppy will do it to help reinforce the command.

As you go through this process, do not start to feel discouraged if the puppy is not sitting down the first time you do it. Some puppies don't realize what is going on and that they need to lower their butt to get the treat. But patience and persistence are the best way for you to get them to start listening to you. If the puppy starts to give up on the treat and doesn't seem like they are focused any longer, saying their name or using a kissy noise can be a good way to get their attention back on you.

Lay Down

After you and your puppy have worked on the sit command for a bit, and the puppy has got this part mastered, it is time to move on to a second command of lay down. You must make sure that the puppy knows how to sit before you start working with the lay down command because if you start teaching them too many commands at once, then you are just going to add in some confusion to the mix.

When the puppy is ready to learn how to lay down, get them to sit in front of you. Next, hold the treat in one hand, and then using the other hand, signal the puppy to lay down by using a hand gesture that had your pointer finger pointing down to the ground in front of the puppy's face. Some of the other steps that you need to use to work on the laying down command include:

1. Put the treat that you are using up to the nose of the puppy and then start to slowly lure the puppy down. You can do this by moving the hand down to the floor, somewhere between their paws. Go at the pace for your dog.

2. Once your hand with the treat hits the floor, slowly move it towards you and away from him along the floor. This motion should be enough to get the dog to lower themselves into a laying position.

3. Once you are able to get the puppy to lay down all of the way, make sure to say the clicker word and give them a treat.

4. Repeat this exercise as many times as you can in the next 15 minutes to help the puppy get the idea down.

Keep in mind with this one that the laying down command is going to force your puppy to focus a bit longer before they are able to get the treat that they want. There are going to be times when the puppy wants to give up before you are able to finish with the final position. Don't get frustrated with this; just keep trying, and your puppy will start to catch on to what you want them to do.

Stay

Teaching your puppy how to stay where you want, even when they want to run off and do something else, is a great training tool that you should work on once the puppy learns how to sit and lay down. It is also a command that can take some time to learn, so bring on the patience. Think of how much self-control you have to teach to a small puppy, and how long they need to maintain their attention span in order to actually stay put when you want them to.

There are different methods that you can use for this one, but sometimes it is easiest to get the puppy to stay when you have them in the lay down position. This means that they are going to be less likely to want to move when they can lay all the way down rather than sitting, but you definitely can teach this command in either position.

The hand position that we need to work with for the stay command is to put your hand up, palm facing the puppy, and fingers together. Think of the hand position that you would use when trying to stop someone from coming towards you. Once you have the hand position and have used the command "stay" to the puppy, the other steps to this process that you need to follow includes:

1. With your hand out, take a step back using both feet.

2. After the two steps back, return back to the position you were at to start.

3. If your puppy was good and stayed seated that entire time, reward them with a treat and with the clicker word.

    a. Keep in mind that this is a puppy, and they probably will not want to stay still. If your puppy does get up before you can return to them, tell them "uh-uh" and get them to go back into the seated position.

    b. For the first few sessions, this may be as far as you are able to get. And that is just fine. The puppy naturally wants to follow you. Just work with them until you can get them to stay seated the whole time.

4. Once the puppy stays seated, try taking two steps back and then returning before the reward and the clicker word.

5. Keep increasing the distance that you decide to walk away from the pup, seeing how long you can go away before they start getting up again. Do this until the puppy starts to understand the command that you are giving them.

6. Repeat this exercise many times until the puppy learns how to stay put.

Wait

After you are done teaching your puppy how to stay, it is time to teach them how to wait. This is a very useful command that you can work with, but often it is underused. It can be applied to teaching your puppy to wait for their food, wait to get their leash off, wait to get out of the crate, and more. It is a great way to teach your puppy a bit of self-control and patience, which is something that all dog owners need at some point or another.

Teaching self-control to the puppy is going to be the key to having a dog that is well trained and can do a great job with all the areas of obedience. Definitely take some time to teach your puppy how to listen to this command. When you are ready to start with, it put the puppy in the position that you would like them to wait in. You may find that sitting or lying down is going to work for this. The best hand signals to use here is to have your pointer finger going up. The steps that you can use to make this happen includes:

1. Tell your puppy to wait and then use the wait hand signal.
2. While the puppy is in the seated position, preferably in the crate where feedings are supposed to happen. Slowly lower the food bowl down to where they can eat.
3. If the puppy sees the bowl of food and starts to jump up or get at the food in other ways, you raise the bowl back up while saying "uh-uh."

4. Get the puppy back into the seated position and then start again. If the puppy is younger or has a lot of energy, you may have to repeat these steps a few times in order to get them to listen to you.

    a. Do not set the bowl of food all the way down until the puppy has actually patiently waited for you to lower it without them getting away from the seated position. Be aware that this can take a bit of time.

5. After you have been able to set the food bowl down, see if you are able to get the puppy to wait for another second, and then say, "OK."

    a. If you see that the puppy starts to go for the food before you say the word "OK," you can tell them "uh-uh" and pick up the bowl before trying again.

    b. "OK" is going to be the release word for your puppy, and it will tell them that it is now fine to stop waiting, and they can eat the food that is in front of them.

    c. As you go through this process, you will want to lengthen the amount of time that the puppy is going to wait between setting the bowl down and saying OK. This takes a bit longer but will get the puppy used to waiting until you give the orders to do something.

Come

The next command that we are going to look at is the one to come. When you do this one, you are going to teach your puppy how to come when you call them.

This is also one that a lot of pet owners are going to forget to teach, and it can lead to some issues with the puppy not listening to you. This is a foundational command that you should work with your puppy on for years to come. You may use it to keep the puppy near you, when there is danger, and more.

Be prepared for this one to take a bit longer than some of the other ones. The puppy has to let you move away from them and then has to move to meet you. There are a number of steps that this will entail working with, but this is a great one to focus your attention on and make sure that you can get them to really listen to you. When you are ready to teach your puppy this command, you can follow these steps:

1. When you are working with this command, make sure that you start out in an enclosed area. This makes it easier in case your puppy decides not to listen because they are limited in the space they have to run away.
2. Take your puppy off the leash and allow them to have some time to just explore and roam around.
3. When you are ready, say the name of the puppy and then use the command "Come" in a positive voice, while also holding on to a treat.
    a. Keep in mind that you want to associate this command with positivity.
    b. Your goal is to get the dog to come every time that you call them. For this to happen, the puppy needs to be conditioned to think that something positive is going to happen when they come to you.

4. If your puppy doesn't end up coming over to you right away, that is fine. You can make some kissy noises or do another thing that will get their attention to make sure that they see the treat that you are offering. Be patient here and work on redirecting the attention of the puppy until he comes to you.

5. When the puppy does come to you, make sure that you reward them with the treat, as well as the clicker word. Do this even if it took a long time for the puppy to make their way over to you. They did listen, even if it took longer than you wanted.

6. Repeat this exercise many times until the puppy starts to come right over to you.

Leave It

The next command that we need to take a look at is "leave it." This can be a beneficial command to train your puppy, considering that they often like to be adventurous and get into everything. When you decide to use this command when the puppy is heading towards something that you don't want them to be in, you are going to see some great results. As the puppy wants to explore and see things, there are many times when this kind of command is going to be a good one to use.

Now, there are going to be a few methods that you are able to use when it comes to the command of "leave it." The first method is going to follow the steps below to make things happen.

1. Any time that the puppy starts to go for or is already into something that you want them to leave alone, firmly tell the puppy "leave it."

2. Remember to only tell them the command once. You can use their name or another sound to get their attention.

3. If you find that the puppy is not responding to this, put a treat or some other toy on their nose and lure them over to listening to you.

4. Once the puppy does decide to leave the object, tell them "Yes" and use the clicker word of your choice. A reward is a good way to reinforce this idea, as well.

5. Remember that your reward for this one needs to be really motivating. You are trying to get the puppy to leave something alone that they are interested in. If the reward is not good, then they are more likely to ignore you and go after the other thing.

The above method is going to work well for most puppies, and it is definitely one you can work with. But another option that you may want to try working with as well depending on your puppy and whether or not they respond to the first method is the second method we will tell you about below:

1. Have the puppy start this training session by lying down.

2. Put down a treat on the ground, covering it by your hand if necessary.

3. Tell your pup to "leave it."

4. Once the puppy looks at you rather than the treat, tell them "Yes" and reward them with the treat from the other hand.

5. Remember, you need to practice this one a bit. It is going to help the dog realize that if they leave the first thing, they are going to get something better, which makes them respond better to you.

Touch

Touch can be a great command to work with, and it is almost like a trick that you are able to do with your puppy. Touch is going to be a great way to teach your puppy to target something and then touch it with their nose. It is a good way to get the brain of your puppy to move and even to keep their focus when it is needed. Some of the steps that you are going to be able to use in order to teach your puppy how to respond to the touch command will include:

1. Make sure that you sit down with the puppy facing you.

2. Hold a treat or some other reward in your one hand.

3. Command your dog to "Touch" and then hold out the hand that doesn't have the treat, so it is flat in front of the nose of your dog while holding onto the treat in the other hand.

a. Once the puppy starts to get the hang of this kind of command, it will no longer be necessary to have the treat in your hand, and you can just put the hand where you would like.

4. In the beginning, you want to put the touching hand six inches or so away from the nose of your dog.

5. As soon as you are able to get the nose of your dog to touch your hand, you can reward him with the treat you have and the clicker word you choose to use.

6. You should never give your dog the treat in the hand that you want them to touch.

7. If you find that the dog is getting the hang of this trick pretty quickly, you can remove the treat and no longer use it at all.

8. As you progress with your puppy, keep moving your touching hand higher above the nose of your dog, adding in a bit of difficulty with it.

Shake

Now we are going to move a bit more into some of the different tricks that you are able to do when you work with your puppy. But the way that you do this is going to be pretty similar to the commands that we were doing before. Think of how much fun it is going to be when you want to get your puppy to shake your hand.

You will find that most puppies are going to take some time to learn how to do this trick. But if you have already spent some time teaching them some of the other commands, it may be a bit easier. As always, your job is to be patient and persistent with this and work on it each day until your puppy is ready to go with it. Some of the steps that you are able to use in order to teach your puppy how to shake with you include:

1. Make sure that you begin this with the puppy facing you.
2. Use the command "shake" and make the shake hand gesture with your hand out, palm out, and waiting.
3. Place the treat right up to one side of your pup's chest.
   a. This one is going to take a bit of patience and can be harder for the puppy to figure out what exactly you want them to do.
   b. Most pups are going to try to bite at the treat and will take some extra pains in order to get to the treat.
4. As soon as the puppy starts to paw at the treat, or even if they just start to lift the paw, immediately reward them with the treat and the clicker word.

For this kind of exercise, if you find that your pup is standing up and getting out of the seated position that you put them in, this is fine. Once they figure out that they are able to get the reward when they lift up their paw, they will figure out that it is easier for them to lift up the paw while they are seated. However, when you first start with this exercise, begin it with the puppy in the seated position before you begin.

Heel

The next command that is on our list is going to be heel. Teaching your puppy how to heel can be one of the most beneficial skills that you can teach them. If you are able to focus on this command with them when they are young, they will know how to behave when you get them older. One big behavioral problem that can happen with a puppy or dog when they get older is that they will pull on the leash while walking. Teaching your puppy how to heel is going to avoid this issue and can make walking a bit easier.

Before we get into some of the steps that we need to take in order to teach your puppy how to heel, we need to look at some tips for loose leash walking. First, remember to work with positive reinforcement. You also want to walk with a leash that is loose and never tighten it because this puts some strain on either end of the leash. You also should consider being as consistent as possible with what side your puppy needs to walk on. Pick a side and keep them there.

With these two things in mind, it is time to see how you can teach your puppy when and how to heel at the right time. The steps to making this happen will include:

1. Position the leash, so it is on your arm or wrist, but make sure that it is still a bit loose.

2. If you have the puppy on the right side, make sure to hold onto the end of the leash with your left hand, and grab it with the right hand down by your side. If you are holding onto the puppy on the left side, then you can flip these instructions around.

3. If you find that the puppy will stay near your side the whole time, then the second hand on the leash won't be necessary.

4. Get into a position where your puppy is on the side that you choose, and then get their attention.

5. Your goal with this one, if you can, is to get the puppy to be as calm and focused as possible so that they can pay attention to the command that you use. Have the puppy sit by you and then reward with the treat and the clicker word.

6. Say the name of your puppy and then ask them to "heel." Keep looking at the puppy as you continue to walk.

7. Any time that the puppy looks up at you, you should say the clicker word. Depending on how often the puppy looks at you, you can provide them with a treat with the clicker word or just on occasion.

   a. The more that you see the puppy look up at you, the less you should reward with a treat so that you can slowly wean off this.

8. When it is time, take one step forward and see if you can get the attention of your puppy. Ideally, they are going to stay next to you and will heel rather than trying to pull forward.

a. If you find that the puppy is losing their focus on you at any time, say their name or use the kissy noise, but never repeat the command more than once.

b. If the puppy keeps the focus on you and the leash is loose, keep on walking. If the puppy tightens the leash and pulls forward, then stop with the walking.

9. Your goal here is to get the puppy to walk back over to you and get the leash loose. If the puppy doesn't do this, say their name and get their attention. If they still don't come back to you, take a step back, and see if the puppy will follow you. Last case scenario that they aren't listening to you, then lure them back with a treat.

10. Once the puppy is back to you again, use the clicker word and offer a treat. Repeat this exercise a bunch of times until the puppy is able to learn how to listen to you and do what you are asking with the heeling.

You want to make sure that with this one that you are picking out a treat that your puppy really likes. Your goal with heel is to teach the puppy how to listen to you and stop moving or pulling on the leash. This means that the reward needs to be greater than whatever else may be catching their attention at the time. Go all out with this one and pick out some of the best treats to get the puppy to listen to you.

There are some puppies who struggle with heel because they are resistant to working with the leash. If this is your puppy, then you should consider working with a harness when teaching the puppy how to heel, and even when you want to introduce them to leash walking in general. Most puppies and older dogs are going to respond to the harness so much better than using the leash for heeling, and for working with the leash for walking in any form.

There are a lot of different commands that you are able to work with when it is time to teach your puppy how to listen to you. Most of these are critical commands that can get the puppy to listen to what you want them to do and to keep them out of harm, though a few of them can be almost like fun tricks that you can do together. Make sure that you take your time and go at the speed that works the best for your puppy. They will learn if you are consistent with the treats and continue doing the rewards and the clicker word each time that they succeed in doing what you would like.

Chapter 9: Dealing with Separation Anxiety

Separation anxiety is a big problem that some dogs will deal with. This is when your dog will get stressed or upset when you try to leave them anywhere. A dog that has this issue is going to cry, howl, bark, pace, destroys objects, has some accidents in the house, or wants to get out of the crate. It is possible that some of these behaviors are learned, and they are going to act out badly because you as the owner allowed it. How are you supposed to know the difference between separation anxiety and bad behaviors?

If you have a puppy that is truly dealing with separation anxiety, you will notice that they are actually going through some emotional stress any time that you leave. If the puppy is just barking to get what they want or for attention, then this is not really separation anxiety at all. This is why it is important to know if there is separation anxiety or if it is a learned behavior because the course of action that you take with each one is going to make a big difference.

When your puppy already has true separation anxiety, then this is something that you are able to work with. It is going to take some time, but it is something that is manageable when you use the right approach to take care of the issue. You will find, though, that each case of separation anxiety is unique. There is no one concrete answer out there about what is going to cause anxiety, and it can be caused by a few different genetic and environmental factors. Some factors that can cause this anxiety will include:

1. Some of the things that may have happened to the puppy in the past before you got them.

2. How long you leave them all on their own each day.

3. Was the puppy trained in the crate properly? If you don't associate the crate with a lot of positivity, then the puppy could have some anxiety about being in it.

4. How the owner responds to some of the unwanted behaviors that the puppy tries to use.

Of course, there are also some puppies that are just going to be more attached to their owners when they are young, and this makes them more likely to develop this separation anxiety. Working through this is going to be a bit different process for each puppy depending on the circumstances and some of the behaviors that come with the dog. Before we get into that, though, we need to take a look at some of the most common mistakes that dog owners are often going to make that can encourage the separation anxiety to get worse. Some of these mistakes that you need to avoid include:

Rewarding Behaviors That You Don't Want

The most common reason why a puppy is going to develop learned behaviors that are not separation anxiety is that the owner rewarded unwanted behaviors rather than good behaviors. In fact, without even knowing what they were doing, many times the owners would feed into the bad behaviors that their puppy was using.

Think about how you react when the puppy is whining or crying? Do you ask them what is the matter and act sympathetic for what they are doing? When they bark to get attention, are you likely to give in to the barking and give them the attention that they want? As an owner, it is likely that you are going to respond to these behaviors in a way that is bad at least a few times.

To reverse what you are doing here, you need to remember that you have to reward the good behaviors, and ignore, or correct, the bad behaviors. If your puppy is dealing with bad behaviors that make them whine and bark when you leave, learning how to ignore these and work just with rewarding the good behaviors is going to make a big difference in how they respond to you.

Making the Greetings and Goodbyes Too Long

Another common method that owners are going to make the separation anxiety worse with their puppy is making greetings and goodbyes too long or too big of a deal. Think about how you act when you get home. Do you ever greet the dog in an excited way and talk to them in a higher voice? It is likely that you are excited to see your puppy after being gone all day long, but making this big of a deal out of being reunited with them is going to really make the separation anxiety that your puppy is feeling so much worse.

This means that if you want to make sure that your puppy remains calm when you come home, you need to be calm as well during both of these times. Make the greetings and farewells less important so that the puppy stays calm as well. You can say hi to them and see them, but you need to do it in a calm manner to keep them relaxed as well.

Leaving the Puppy Alone in a Bad Environment

And finally, another bad mistake that a lot of dog owners will do is to put the dog in a poor environment. It can also matter how you introduce this kind of place to your puppy. Often leaving the puppy in the crate is going to be the best, but we want to make this a place of comfort, and not one that the puppy is going to feel punished in. Plus, if you leave the puppy there for eight hours or longer a day while you are at work, then you need to make sure that you let them out to play, run around outside, and explore so they aren't in the crate all of the time.

Dealing with separation anxiety is going to be really hard to work with in some cases, but there are a few different things that you are able to work with in order to help prevent it. To help your puppy not gain anxiety based on the crate they are in all day, you should allow the puppy to get used to the crate when you are actually home, along with the times when you are gone. If the puppy sees the crate as a good place, as a place they can call their own and relax in, whether you are home or not, they are less likely to have anxiety when they are put inside of it.

Allow your puppy to explore the crate when you are home. This helps the puppy to see the crate as a good place, rather than them associating the crate with being left alone. This is a practice that makes the dog realize that just because they have to go into the crate and you are leaving, does not mean that each time they do that they are going to be left alone for a long time.

For example, if you start out this process by putting the puppy into the crate for shorter periods of time, such as when you run out to get the mail or just walk around the block, it is slowly going to condition the puppy so that they grow more comfortable with the time they spend in the crate. As they get accustomed to the crate and being alone for the shorter periods, you can then work to increase the amount of time they are in this crate. Go from getting the mail to running some short errands and so on until you are gone for the eight hours.

While you can't avoid the fact that you need to go to work and the puppy will have to stay in the crate for longer periods of time, the idea with this is that with some of the shorter periods of time added into it, the puppy is not going to feel so worked up before you leave. They are less likely to feel like you will be gone forever each time that you try to put them into the crate.

As a final reminder here, separation anxiety is going to be a long process that some owners will need to work on over the entire span of the life of the dog. This can be frustrating and discouraging if you want to go with a fix that is a bit quicker, but it is the best way to keep your cool and calm, and to ensure that you keep working on it for the good of the puppy and the good of your own sanity as well.

Another thing that can sometimes cause some of this separation anxiety is if a major change happens in the life of the puppy. When these happen, they can cause some forms of separation anxiety even in a dog that never showed signs of this in the past. And sometimes situations that may not seem like a big deal to us as humans are going to be enough to challenge the puppy and make them feel this kind of anxiety.

If you notice that your puppy is starting to show signs of being anxious when you leave, especially if they were not like this before, then it is time to take a look at what changes may be happening in their world, and what you can fix. It may be a simple change that you barely noticed, but it made a big deal to the puppy. Fixing it and getting them accustomed to the change, or removing the change if it is not that important to you, can help the puppy be more comfortable and get back to their old way of doing things.

There are a lot of changes that can happen in the life of your puppy that may cause them to deal with separation anxiety in the process. There could be a change in routine, a move to a new home, or a new owner. Remember that all three of those are going to show up when you try to bring your puppy home for the first time. Being patient and thinking about the needs of your puppy, and learning how to work through the separation anxiety is going to make life easier for both of you.

Separation anxiety is going to show up at different times for each puppy, and it is going to depend on the puppy that you have, their personality, and some of the life experiences that they may have had in the past. You may find that the anxiety can start as early as when you walk through the door with a new puppy, or a big life change later on could be the root cause that you have to deal with. Understanding this and looking for some of the signs of separation anxiety will make a difference.

You are able to prevent some of the separation anxiety that your puppy is feeling just by avoiding some of the mistakes that we have talked about in this chapter. The thing to remember here, even if you are following the advice that is above, is that there are some puppies that will come to your home with a very attached personality, and they may need to go through some extra socialization and steps in order to prevent the anxiety from starting in the first place.

If you find that your puppy is like this, and some of the symptoms that come with separation anxiety start to show up, you may find that having your puppy go to a dog daycare, or having someone come over during the day to play with and walk to your puppy can help. This helps the puppy to get a lot of socialization and can be the best way to help them realize that you are not the only person in the world. Often just a bit of time with this is enough to help the puppy get over their issues with separation anxiety.

This doesn't have to be an all the time thing. Even just one day of dog daycare for your puppy is enough to give them the socialization that they need and can get them out of the house rather than being alone. Doing this once a week for a few months can help the puppy see that they are not alone, even when you leave, and will make it easier for your puppy to get out some of that pent up energy from being home waiting for you all day too.

Separation anxiety is an issue that some dog owners are going to need to deal with when they bring a new puppy home. Some dogs will not have this issue, and others are going to find that it is something major that they need to deal with. Before you jump in and try to make things better for the puppy, make sure that you are dealing with the true separation anxiety and not just some bad behaviors where the puppy is trying to get what they want or to get your attention.

Once you have determined that your puppy is actually dealing with separation anxiety, you can take the steps that are needed to help put a stop to it. Understanding the changes that are going on with your puppy, learning how to be calmer when you leave and come home, and teaching the puppy about the crate in a more positive manner, so they don't feel worried when you leave them in there, are all important. When all of this comes together, you will find that it is much easier for you to get your puppy to feel comfortable and safe, and to stop some of the separation anxiety when you leave, even when they have to be home alone for some time.

Chapter 10: Tough Dog Problems and How to Deal with Them

Once you are able to train your dog a few of the commands from the last chapter you will find that the puppy is going to behave the way that you would like. They will listen to the commands that you give and will get along with the family. However, each puppy is going to have a different kind of personality and it is possible that they will still deal with some problems that you will need to take care of.

Some puppies are not going to have any of these tough dog problems, and some are going to have a few that you need to deal with. Learning what your puppy is going to do when others come around, and what behaviors you need to fix and fixing them as quickly as possible, can be the key to having a puppy behave the way that you want. Some of the most common tough dog problems that your puppy may show and the steps you can take to deal with them include:

Jumping up on Other People

Do you find that your puppy likes to jump up on you and other people? For those who know what this is like, know that this is actually a behavior issue that should not be encouraged. Owners find that it can be hard to get dogs, no matter the age, to stop jumping up on them and some of the other people who are around them. Even if you don't feel like this is a big deal right now, think about how you are going to feel about the dog jumping on you or someone else when they are 100+ pounds? It is better to train your puppy to not jump on anyone from a young age. It is easier this way and ensures that they aren't going to be toppling other people over either.

First, we need to take a look at why the puppy is likely to jump on you or other people. For the most part, this is because they are excited. They see you or someone else come through the door and because they don't have the necessary self-control yet, and they want to jump up to show how excited they are to see you. Or, there may be times when the puppy is going to jump up because they see some item in your hand that they want, and they jump up to try and get it.

Either way, it is important to learn how to stop the puppy from jumping up on you and knocking you and others down. You need to remember to be consistent. You can't discourage the jumping one day and then be excited to see them another day and be fine with the jumping. Also, you can't have your cake and eat it too. You can't allow the dog to jump on you, and then train them not to jump on other people. This confuses the puppy and won't help you or them out at all.

You have to decide that the jumping is a bad behavior, and then work to train them not to do it.

The good news here is that you are able to follow a simple process in order to get your puppy to listen to you and do what you would like. As with all of the unwanted behaviors that we are going to bring up in this chapter, you need to be strict about not allowing the puppy to jump on you ever. As you are going through the training process, and you see that the puppy is trying to jump on you, use the following steps to help prevent the behavior:

1. Tell the puppy, "OFF."

2. Turn your body around so that your puppy is looking directly at your back.

3. When you move the body so that it is turned around, the puppy is going to automatically get their paws back down on the floor and where they should be.

4. After the puppy has put their paws down, you can turn to face the puppy and then redirect them until they are sitting down.

5. Once the puppy listens and actually sits down, pet them, and reward them, showing the puppy that this is the way you want them to get your attention.

6. Now, there are going to be some times when the puppy will attempt to jump up on you again. If they start to do this, stop providing them with attention, and go through the steps above again. Only give the puppy some attention and affection when they are sitting down.

7. Practice with this each time that you come into the house, and even purposely leave for a few minutes so that you get some more practice. Over time, this is going to become a habit, and the puppy will learn that they are not supposed to jump on you.

The point of doing this is to show the puppy that they are only going to get attention when they sit, rather than getting any attention when they are up and moving and jumping on others. This will help stop them from jumping on you and can do some wonders for teaching them some self-control along the way.

Destructive Chewing

Another issue that a lot of puppies will fall into is that they will start to chew on a lot of things that they shouldn't, many items that you do not allow, and are not part of their chew toys. When you first bring a puppy home, especially if they are only about eight weeks old, remember that they don't know what is and what is not allowed to chew on. You have to step up and teach them these rules. Sure, it is easy to get frustrated with the puppy when they chew on the wrong thing, but you have to be proactive and teach your puppy what is appropriate behavior, especially when it comes to chewing.

While it may feel like the puppy is purposely being naughty and just had to go after your favorite pair of shews, remember that there are a lot of reasons why the puppy is chewing in the first place. They aren't trying to be naughty, and they aren't trying to make life more difficult for you. Some of the reasons that your puppy may be chewing on things include:

1. Dogs have a need that is instinctual that tells them to chew on things.
2. Chewing is a good outlet for most puppies when it is time to exert energy. Your dog could be chewing on a variety of items when they have a lot of energy that they need to get rid of, or when they feel a bit bored with their activities.
3. Similar to what we see with infants, puppies like to put objects into their mouths in the hopes of figuring out what the object is, and what they should do with it.
4. Puppies will often chew when they are teething. This chewing method is going to be a good way for them to soothe their gums.

Your dog is going to chew, and they need to chew, no matter if they are a brand new puppy or you have had them around for some time. You can't stop them from chewing, but you can control what they are allowed to do this with. You just need to pick out the right chew toys or items that you are going to give to the puppy and teach them what they can chew on, and what they need to avoid.

The good news is there are a few things that you are able to do in order to make sure the puppy is going to chew on the right items, and that they won't start to chew on some of your favorite items or on anything that they shouldn't have their mouths on. Some of the rules that you are able to follow when it comes to this include:

1. Always have some approved chewing objects that you can give to your puppy. Your puppy is going to chew no matter what, so make sure that you provide them with some toys or objects that they are allowed to chew on instead of getting mad when they chew on items that you don't approve of.

2. Be strict with what they can chew on, and what they can't chew on. In the beginning, you have to be strict on this and may have to keep the puppy confined to one area. But this is their learning period, and you are going to see the best results when you can keep track of the puppy and make sure that they don't get ahold of things they shouldn't have.

3. Redirect the puppy to an object that you approve of for them to chew on. The puppy is sometimes going to get away from you and will try to chew on something that they should not. When you catch them in the act, don't try to shout or yell or get mad about it. This just encourages them because the puppy sees that they are getting attention from this. Instead, when you find them, say "NO" and then redirect them over to an item that is designed for them to chew on.

Pulling on the Leash

Another common issue that you will see when you bring home a new puppy is that they like to pull on the leash. This one seems to be a really hard problem for most dog owners to deal with, and it seems like most owners are going to allow their puppy to pull on the leash forever. The good news is that it is possible to train your puppy to stop pulling on the leash, making things a whole lot easier for you.

The bottom line to remember here is that your leash should never be tight when you try to take the puppy on a walk. A loose leash is going to be the standard that you set, and it means that there is a little bit of slack on the leash between the puppy and you. There are a few reasons why you would want this to happen. It is going to teach the puppy that you are the pack leader and they should respect you. You don't want the puppy to start to think that they get to lead you all the time. When the puppy decides to make the leash tight and pulls on it, it is going to add a ton of stress and pressure to the neck, and this can be harmful to them. Pulling can also cause some damage to your own joints on the shoulders and arms. And when the puppy goes with a loose leash, it is going to become a much more enjoyable walk for both of you.

Now, this brings up the question of what you are supposed to do when the puppy decides to pull on the leash when you are walking. This may slow down your walk a bit, but you will find that most puppies are going to catch on quick, and doing this can really make a difference in how well the walk goes. Taking some time now will help you have much more pleasant walks overall. Some of the steps that you are able to do to help stop the puppy from pulling on the leash will include:

1. Any time that you feel the dog is getting excited and starts pulling on the leash, stop right where you are and don't go any further.

2. When the puppy starts to see that you have stopped and looks back at you, work with the clicker word.

3. Wait for the puppy to walk back to you, and when the puppy does this, reward them with a treat.

4. If you notice that the puppy is not coming back to you, lure them back using the heeling position and with a treat if you need it.

5. Now, there are some times when the puppy is still not going to come over to you. If this is the case, you can take another step back. Continue to do this until the puppy starts to walk back to you.

6. Repeat this process as many times as you need during the walk until the puppy learns that the leash needs to be loose.

As you can imagine, this is going to slow down the walk for a bit. You may only want to go on a walk down the block or so until the puppy starts to get the hang of what you are doing. The good news here is that the puppy will learn, and you will get the puppy to walk alongside you, with a nice loose leash rather than one that is tight and harming both you and the puppy, in no time.

The Puppy Doesn't Want to Walk on the Leash

There are some puppies who are so excited to go on a walk that they will bounce around, and then, once you are outside, they are going to pull on the leash, and you need to work on that problem. But then there are the puppies that don't like to walk on the leash at all. This is common for puppies who haven't been exposed to the leash at all. Most of the time they are going to catch on pretty quickly though, you just need to do a few steps in order to make this work for you. Some of the steps that you can use to get your puppy more used to the leash and doing what you want with it include:

1. Pull on the leash a bit, gently to the side while telling the command of "come" to the puppy.

2. If you find that this is not working, then call the puppy to you with a treat or something else that can be a reward.

3. If neither of the two steps above are working, you can try it with a harness and just repeat the steps that we have from above.

a. You will find that the harness can be a nice addition because it gives you a bit more control over the puppy while making it so that you don't put too much pressure on the neck of your puppy.

4. Once the puppy listens to you and walks over, reward the puppy with a treat and a clicker word.

5. If you find that the puppy is responding pretty well with this, try calling the puppy to you without the treat, and use the clicker word on its own as a reward.

6. Repeat the process again until your puppy gets more familiar with the leash and doesn't seem to mind it as much.

Too Much Roughhousing with the Puppy

You will find that in some instances, your puppy is going to get into a really crazy mood where they will zoom around so much that they end up losing their self-control and won't behave well. When a puppy is in this kind of state, you will find that redirecting the puppy is not going to be enough. The more excitement that the puppy has, the harder it is to get the puppy to control themselves. This means that you need to step up and gain control before the puppy has their energy escalate too high.

This is going to require the whole family getting on board and making sure they are all on the same page. If the kids are working to rile the puppy up, it could get out of control before you even have a chance to slow it down a bit. The sooner you are able to slow the puppy down; the easier things are going to be for you.

What this means is if you see that the excitement of the puppy is starting to build, it is time to gain control right away. You can have them sit or do one of the other commands that gets them to stop and listen to you. Sitting is a good way to force the puppy to have some self-control and calm down.

Now, there may be some times when the puppy is going to be in this state already. This means that the puppy is going to have already lost their self-control, and you and the rest of the family may need to remove yourselves from the situation so that they don't exert this loss of control onto the kids or you at this time. Another option that can work with this is to put the dog in the leash and take them outside to wear out some of that energy or let them run in the backyard. This helps to get some of that pent up energy out, and then the puppy will be able to exert the self-control again.

Fearfulness

There are some puppies who are going to be more reserved and may have some fears of the world, or at least a fear of things that are unfamiliar. It is natural to want to shelter them from the things that they fear, but this actually is going to cause the puppy more harm than good. The key in cases of fearfulness is to try and expose the puppy to the things that they are afraid of, but you should do it in a positive, as well as in a gradual, manner.

If you notice that you have a puppy that seems to be afraid of trying out anything new, or they have some fears that they can't seem to get over, there are a few steps that you can try out including:

1. Give your puppy some exposure to the thing that they are afraid of. Do this in a very slow manner so that they have time to look it over and explore it.

2. Start out with a big distance between the object the puppy is scared of and the puppy itself.

3. Associate the object of the puppy's fear with a lot of positivity. A good way to do this is to add something that the puppy really likes or really loves into that situation.

4. If your puppy is motivated by food, make sure that they are given a lot of treats while you expose them to that object.

5. Slowly start to move the puppy a bit closer to the object that they are scared about. Let them have some time to gain comfort with each distance to the object.

a. Keep in mind that slowly is going to vary based on the puppy and how they are reacting to this process. You have to go at the speed and the distance that works the best for your puppy.

b. If you find that the puppy seems pretty comfortable and unstressed, you may be able to approach the object of their fear on that same day. But for some puppies, moving them just a bit closer each day is going to be the best option.

You will need to repeat this process again and again, going a bit closer each day, until the puppy has been able to overcome their fears. Throughout the whole process, make sure to pay attention to the body language of the puppy, and learn their signals. You do not want to have them become too stressed out, and you don't want to push the puppy past their limits because this is just going to make things worse, and the puppy will start to fear the object more than before.

The Escape Artist

Hopefully you are able to read this part of the guidebook before the puppy has been able to escape out of your home and run away. Obviously, having the puppy escape and get lost is a traumatic experience for the whole family. But if the puppy is able to do this once, then it is likely they will continue to do this again and again.

There are several reasons why the puppy is going to try and get out of the home. They are allowed to roam freely, get into things, and do anything that they want. When they are out of the home, and away from you, they don't have to follow any of the rules any longer! Escaping is going to be a kind of self-rewarding behavior for a dog, and because of this fact, it is going to be a hard one to break if the puppy has already been able to do this.

This means that your goal needs to be to prevent the puppy from getting out and escaping from the home in the first place. Some of the steps that you can take to help prevent your dog from bolting or escaping from your home will include:

1. Make sure that you are fully aware of where your dog is each time that you are about to go out the door. Make sure that all of the people in the home, even visitors, are aware of this kind of rule.

2. Train your dog to sit and consistently wait before going outside can be useful for this, as well. It may take a bit more time and patience, and it is likely that the dog won't want to do it, but it helps them to know they have to sit still if they want to go out.

3. If your back yard has a fence, then you need to make sure that it is secure in every place. You do not want to have any places on the fence or in the yard where your puppy will be able to get through.

4. If you do not have a fenced in back yard, then you need to make sure that the puppy is always on a leash.

The last point that is up above is going to be important. You may be tempted to keep the puppy off the leash because they have been behaving and have not been getting off the leash lately. But this gives the puppy a perfect chance to escape. You have to be consistent with this so that the puppy will know their boundaries.

Too Much Whining and Barking

You will find that an excessive amount of barking is going to be a really frustrating behavioral issue that you, as a new owner of a puppy, will have to deal with. This is also one of the biggest stressors that come up with a dog and their owner. This is why it is so important to solve the problem before it gets to a level that is too hard to control.

First, you need to be able to understand why the puppy is barking so much in the first place. Some of the reasons why your puppy may be barking so much to start with will include:

1. To try and get your attention
2. Because they are uncertain or fearful about something.
3. They want to be able to assert their own dominance over a passerby or another animal.

There are different steps that you will need to take based on what the puppy is barking at. If you find that the puppy is barking at you at this time, then it is because they want to gain more control, or they want your attention. Whether your puppy wants to be with the rest of the pack or they need some more exercise or something else, this is a behavior that you need to correct right away. The steps that you can take to make this work include:

1. If you notice that the puppy continues to bark, turn your back to them and continue to ignore them until they stop.

2. Have some patience here because the puppy is going to continue their barking, in some cases, for a long period of time.

3. Once the puppy does stop barking, no matter how long it took, you can turn around and give the puppy lots of praise, treats, and attention.

4. Any time that the puppy starts to bark at you, repeat this process until they stop barking. This lets them know that you will only give them attention if they are not barking.

5. If you can't get the puppy to stop barking, then it is time to take a break in the crate until they are all done.

In some cases, the puppy is going to bark at passerby and animals. This issue is sometimes embarrassing when you bring your puppy in public, but some people may feel a bit frightened if they don't know your dog. Many times, the owner is going to reinforce this behavior by screaming at the puppy to stop. You need to shift up the way that you respond to the barking first to get them to listen.

Let's say that the puppy is barking when they look at people or dogs through the window. Some of the steps that you are able to use in order to get the puppy to stop barking in this manner include:

1. Call the puppy's name in a positive manner so that they put their focus on you instead of the object of their attention outside.
2. The positive aspect of this is going to be the most important thing that you can do, but it is often the hardest as well. You need to find a way to be more motivating to the puppy than what they see outside.
3. Once the puppy does look over at you, reward them before refocusing their attention on something else that they like, such as a bone or a toy, so they don't get distracted again and start barking.

It is also possible that your puppy is going to start barking at some people and other animals when they are in public. You are not going to be able to demand that they listen to you in the same manner that you could when at home. But this also doesn't mean that you have to just let the puppy bark all day long while you are out in public, or that you have to go home. When you have a puppy who is barking at people and other animals when they are out in public, some of the steps that you can take include:

1. If you have a puppy who is already barking, it is time to move far enough away from the focus of their bark so that they stop the barking. If you are aware of a stimulus that may cause the puppy to bark, try to start out far enough away so that they aren't going to bark at it to start with.

2. When the puppy is looking in the direction of the stimuli, call their name and do what it takes to redirect their focus back on you. When the puppy looks at you, give them a treat. This is going to help them to associate that stimulus with positivity.

3. As you get the puppy to self-control and calm down, see if you are able to move a bit closer to the stimuli. With each step, stop and redirect the puppy back to you, and get them to gain the self-control that you want.

   a. The degree you move is going to vary between each animal, so take your time and see what works for your dog.

4. During this process, make sure that you are the one who is maintaining the control, not the dog. Check on a regular basis that the puppy remains relaxed during this process.

5. If you move closer and your puppy starts to bark again, it is time to move further away and then work to focus their attention back onto you before trying again.

Being on the Furniture

If you do not want the puppy to get up on your furniture, then this is another problem that you will need to work on as soon as possible. Remember that this one is up to you. Some people don't mind the puppy being on the furniture, and some don't want the puppy there at all. Either one is fine as long as you are consistent all the way.

For those who don't want their puppy on the furniture for one reason or another, this is just fine, but you need to start early, be firm with your decision, and be consistent. It isn't going to work if you sometimes allow the puppy on the furniture, and then other times, they are not allowed up there. It also will not work if you tell the puppy not to get on the furniture, but then others in the family allow the puppy to get up there.

If you have decided that you do not want to have your puppy to be up on the furniture, some of the steps that you are going to take in order to make sure that the puppy will stay off your furniture include:

1. Be strict right from the start and make sure that the puppy is never allowed on the furniture.
2. Any time that the puppy tries to jump up on the furniture, tell them "OFF."
3. Motivate the puppy to get off of your furniture and back to the floor by drawing them down with a treat or a toy.

a. If you find that the puppy is not really willing to get off the furniture with this, then it is fine to guide the puppy down with the use of their collar to follow your No.

4. Make sure to reward the puppy with praise, a treat, and the clicker word when they do get off the furniture. Remember, with this one that prevention is going to be the best way to work through the behavior, and if you find that the puppy is heading for the couch, be ahead of the game and automatically direct them to sit and give them a reward in the process.

Digging

While this is not really a behavior that is going to be bad for the puppy, it can be harmful to your yard, and this may be the reason that you stop it. Of course, most people don't want to look out in their yard and see a bunch of holes everywhere, so dealing with this problem right from the start can really help.

The first thing that we need to look at here is some of the reasons that a dog is going to dig. Each dog will be a bit different, but generally, a dog is going to dig because their breed has a genetic disposition to digging, they are using this to help them get their energy out, or they feel bored.

This is one of those times when it is best to be preventative to make sure the puppy does not dig. Exercising and stimulating your puppy can help them to not get bored, and it gets all of that extra energy out so that they are not likely to dig in your yard any longer. A puppy who is exerting all of their energy with playing with their toys, chewing on bones, and getting out on walks is going to find that they have no need to go to the yard and dig some holes. If genetics are the problem, then there probably isn't much that you can do preventatively with this one. You just need to learn how to correct the behavior to get it to stop with your puppy.

If you do happen to catch the dog digging in your yard and you want to get them to stop, there are a few steps that you are able to take. Some of these steps include:

1. If you find that your dog is already digging in your yard, tell them "NO" in a firm manner and get them away and distracted from the hole.
   a. If you can, immediately redirect him to an appropriate item he can exert his energy into, such as running around the yard or chewing on a bone.
2. If you find a new hole that you didn't catch your puppy digging, there is nothing that you should do about the behavior. You need to make sure that you catch them in the act. If it is after the fact, then you are out of luck.
   a. Remember that you are not able to discipline the puppy for something they did that you weren't able to catch them doing.

b. Your puppy is not going to remember that they dug the hole, even if it was just a minute ago. Scolding the puppy later on, is not going to do you any good because the puppy won't have any idea what you are scolding them for.

As you can see, there are a lot of behaviors that your puppy may show off that are going to make life a bit harder when you are working with your puppy. It is best if you are able to be proactive with this process and learn how to deal with the behaviors before they get even worse. The sooner that you are able to deal with these problems, the easier it is going to be. Following the steps that are in this chapter will make it easier for you to really get your puppy to behave in the manner that you would like.

Conclusion

Thank you for making it through to the end of *Puppy Training*. Let's hope it was informative and able to provide you with all of the tools you need to achieve your goals, whatever they may be.

The next step is to spend some time working with your puppy on some of the training techniques that we brought up in this guidebook. Each puppy is going to learn how to behave in their own way, and some puppies are going to take a bit longer to behave and act the way that you want them to. But this guidebook is going to provide you with the results that you want, and before you know it, your new puppy will be able to respond to the commands that you give and will be fully trained in no time.

This guidebook was meant to be the ultimate guide to helping you really train your puppy and see some amazing results. We looked at the basics of training any command to your puppy, along with some of the specific commands that you are able to train your puppy to respond to. We looked at the importance of a crate for your puppy and how to crate train them. And we even looked at house training them so that they can be accident-free and not messing up your home. When all of this comes together, along with some of the other topics that we look at, your puppy will be trained and ready to go!

When you are trying to prepare for bringing home a new puppy and you want to know the best steps to helping them to behave and follow the commands and rules that you set up in your home, make sure to check out this guidebook to help you get started.

Finally, if you found this book useful in any way, a review on Amazon is always appreciated!